No pain is greater than the pain of loving a prodigal. Each morning you feel you must scratch and claw your way to the lowest level of the peace of Christ. Is there nothing you can do?

Far from nothing, there is something of infinite value; value to you and to the one you so frantically love. You can pray. You can call down power from on high. *Praying Your Prodigal Home* is the story of how one man prayed for his prodigal son, but it is not like the story of Elijah and the prophets of Baal, where in one day the prayers were offered and salvation dropped from heaven like lightning. This is like the story of Abraham, who was promised a blessing but did not see its fulfillment for decades. Richard Burr has learned the power of patient, persistent, prevailing prayer. As a faithful disciple, he is sharing the truth of God's Word with you, filtered through the lens of his own experience. This book is full of grace. It is full of hope. It is a path that can lead both you and your prodigal home.

—Pastor Jay Abramson, Ph.D.
Valley Community Baptist Church

As former prodigals ourselves, we understand the blindness of a prodigal to his own circumstances and the anguish, guilt and sense of helplessness of those who are close to a prodigal. In Richard Burr's *Praying Your Prodigal Home*, he reveals that this situation is not without hope. Rather, God is calling us into action. He stands ready to equip us to be active participants in the spiritual battle for the very souls of the prodigals. Triumphantly, we find that our anguish, guilt and helplessness are transformed into true love for the prodigal, joy in being a part of the will of God and peace in knowing that God is always our hope and strength in a seemingly hopeless situation.

—Elizabeth Shelton, marketing director &
Stephen Shelton, investment banker

A moving account of God's transforming grace in the life of a father and son—written by a tender father who, in honesty, exposes his personal pain.

This gripping story sheds light on the incredible power of intercessory prayer which persistently, and rightly, believes that God accomplishes His good purposes in the lives of those whose names are carried to the throne of grace.

—Bruce Fiol, senior pastor
Marco Presbyterian Church

In *Praying Your Prodigal Home*, you are going to read about practical and down-to-earth ways to reach out to God and to pray for those you love who are living in a "far country."

Be thankful for the book you hold in your hands and for the man who is honest enough and wise enough to write it. But, far more than that, rejoice and be thankful for a God who cares and loves your "prodigal" more than you do.

—Steve Brown
Key Life Ministries, Maitland, Florida

PRAYING

Your

PRODIGAL
HOME

Unleashing God's Power to Set Your Loved Ones Free

RICHARD A. BURR

WingSpread Publishers
Camp Hill, Pennsylvania

3825 Hartzdale Drive · Camp Hill, PA 17011
www.wingspreadpublishers.com

A division of Zur Ltd.

Praying Your Prodigal Home
ISBN: 978-1-60066-128-0
LOC Control Number: 2008923225
© 2003 by Richard A. Burr

Previously published by Christian Publications, Inc.
First Christian Publications Edition 2003
First WingSpread Publishers Edition 2008

Unless otherwise indicated, Scripture taken from the HOLY BIBLE:
NEW INTERNATIONAL VERSION ®. Copyright © 1973, 1978, 1984 by the
International Bible Society. Used by permission of Zondervan Bible Publishers.

Scripture references labeled "NKJV" are taken from the HOLY BIBLE:
NEW KING JAMES VERSION. Copyright © 1979, 1980, 1982 by
Thomas Nelson, Inc. Used by permission.

Scripture references labeled "NASB" are taken from the New American Standard
Bible. © The Lockman Foundation 1960, 1962, 1963, 1968, 1971, 1972, 1975,
1995. A Corporation Not for Profit. La Habra, CA. All rights reserved.

Scripture references labeled "Wuest" are taken from *The New Testament:
An Expanded Translation* by Kenneth S. Wuest. Copyright 1961 by
Wm. B. Eerdman Publishing Co.

*Note: Italicized words in Scripture passages
are the emphasis of the author.*

Behold! The Lamb of God who takes
away the sin of the world!

(John 1:29, NKJV)

Contents

Foreword

Almost all Christians have a prodigal in their life—someone who they desperately want to know the love, peace and salvation that comes with an eternal relationship with our great God and Savior through the atoning death of Jesus Christ. And yet, in spite of all our fervent prayers and attempts to share the truth with these people, they continually reject it, and oftentimes us as well. It is easy to start doubting that they will ever experience what we so deeply wish and pray for them.

It is for this reason that I so highly recommend *Praying Your Prodigal Home*. As one who has both lived as a prodigal and experienced the pain of loving and pursuing a prodigal, Richard Burr has gathered much wisdom on the subject and shares it here in a very clear and readable fashion. His perspectives on the powerful love of God (which makes ours pale in comparison), on how the Holy Spirit draws unbelievers to Himself and other truths will tremendously encourage all who read them.

And yet, this is not simply a book of comfort—Richard presents some hard facts that we need to face. His purpose in writing this book was not to give the reader a warm dose of optimism. It is a call to action—not just to share Christ and represent Him well, but to take our God-given opportunity to pray deeply and much more seriously for our prodigals.

This book is greatly needed, and for this reason I am indebted to Richard Burr. May you benefit from his transparency and wisdom, and may God move through your heart and mind as you read!

—Dr. Bill Bright, founder and chairman
Campus Crusade for Christ

Acknowledgments

The book you are about to read has been one of the most gut-wrenching projects that this writer has ever encountered. For, as you will see, it is punctuated with personal and family anecdotes that have been used to magnify the character, attributes and immutable precepts of God. But, quite frankly, some of the details have been painful to acknowledge publicly. In fact, one who has been privy to some of these events has said, "Less is best." However, my purpose for sharing such personal experiences has not been to elevate man or to expose questionable choices and/or deeds, but to focus exclusively upon the *redemptive power of the gospel in transforming the hearts and lives of wretched sinners—of whom I am the worst.*

It is my prayer that this volume will be *encouraging* to those who have been, or who are presently working their way through, similar straits and to be *instructional* on how to pray effectively for unbelievers. Also, I pray that God would graciously use this book as an *evangelistic* tool to bring multitudes of prodigals to repentance and faith in Christ Jesus.

I am grateful to all those who have assisted me in this labor of love. First, and foremost, is my precious bride, Anastasia (i.e., my living Greek lexicon), who has reviewed and edited this manuscript dozens upon dozens of times for proper syntax, relevancy of the anecdotes and proper interpretation and exposition of Scripture to its original text.

We are deeply indebted to our precious friends and colaborers: Steve Westbrook, who spent many hours editing the original work so that it would be more readable; Dr. Bruce Fiol, Pastor Don Schaeffer and Pastor Michael Elliott, who scrutinized the manuscript for proper theology and biblical references; Dr. Arnold Cheyney, who reviewed the grammar and flow; Dr. Dale and Paige Perrigan, Stephen and Elizabeth Shelton, Dave and Helga Findley, Phyllis Nelson and others who gave many suggestions and much encouragement.

Also, we want to express our gratitude to David Fessenden, our skillful and talented editor, for his most significant contribution to this book.

Finally, we would be remiss if we didn't include all of those who have undergirded this project—and this ministry—with their faithful prayers, unwavering support and sacrificial gifts over these many years! How can we ever thank you enough for the joy you have given us in serving Him?

Thank you all, in the bonds of our Savior's love!

Prologue

oes prayer really change things? Is God really interested in the minutiae of our lives? Or is the Almighty, who controls the movements of galaxies, really concerned with the affairs of us frail creatures of the dust?

Frequently, the evil one takes questions such as these and uses them as weapons to create havoc within our souls by casting doubt upon the very character of our merciful God and also upon the effectiveness of prayer. After years of wrestling with such questions, I am convinced that the primary mission of Satan is to undermine God's people with discouragement, doubt and deception, particularly in the area of prayer. And never have I wrestled with the enemy's lies more fiercely than in the thirty-plus years I have been crying out to the Lord for the spiritual well-being of my three sons and grandchildren.

The great prayer warrior Ole Hallesby wrote, "The secret prayer chamber is a bloody battleground. Here violent and decisive battles are fought out. Here the fate of souls for time and eternity is determined, in quietude and solitude, without another soul as spectator or listener."[1]

I totally agree with Hallesby; prayer is a battleground. And yet, the secret closet of prayer is also a place of refuge—especially for the parents and loved ones of prodigals. When you are hurting and your children are in rebellion, the tendency is to go horizontally—to other people—and you may possibly receive some temporary encouragement that way. But I learned years ago that the key is *not* going horizontally, but going vertically—to God. That is why this book was written—because I believe this is where the battle is going to be won.

The book you are about to read illustrates this raging battle within one family, particularly in the lives of a prodigal father and a prodigal son. It also shows God's ready inclination to relieve the misery of these two fallen creatures by bringing both to repentance and faith in Christ Jesus. Furthermore, it chronicles the precepts you need to know as you enter into the fray for the soul of your prodigal.

It is God's desire to use His people to draw prodigals to Himself, and prayer is the way He has ordained to accomplish this task. Prayer is the ministry above all other ministries; without it we actually limit God's chosen method of work. And when you couple prayer with the Word, they become the chief means by which our Lord grows His Church. This is gloriously demonstrated in the early Church, when the apostles decided, "We will give ourselves continually to prayer and to the ministry of the word," and the result was, "Then the word of God spread, and the number of the disciples multiplied greatly" (Acts 6:4, 7, NKJV).

Every single issue of the Christian life goes back to what Hallesby calls "the bloody prayer chamber," where decisions for all of time and eternity are going to be determined, where they are fought and waged and they are won. But sadly, most Christians have never plumbed the depths of the secret closet of prayer.

In my previous book, *Developing Your Secret Closet of Prayer* (WingSpread Publishers, 1998), my coauthor and I outlined the basic fundamentals for developing intimacy with God through prayer. While we examined several facets of one's prayer life, intercessory prayer was *not* covered, because there was no room for the voluminous material that would have been required. Even in this book, I have limited my discussion to praying for prodigals—unbelievers. Other types of intercessory prayer, which deserve to be covered extensively, may perhaps appear in a future book.

I trust that this book will encourage you and help you to integrate intercessory prayer with the proclamation of the gospel, in the power of the Holy Spirit, as you pray your prodigal home.

The springboard that catapults us into the instructional part of this book is a compelling story of God's divine intervention into a wayward son's final moments of life, reconciling him with his earthly father and, more importantly, with his heavenly Father. God graciously rescued him from the dominion of darkness and supernaturally delivered him into the kingdom of light.

ONE

For this son
of mine was dead
and is
alive again,
he was lost
and is found.

The Prodigal

t was one of those gorgeous Indian summer evenings in western Pennsylvania—Friday, October 29, 1999, to be exact. My wife and I had just finished an exhausting day of chores in preparation for an early Saturday morning departure to western Canada. As we sat down to a late dinner, the telephone rang and the voice of my youngest son, Bruce, gave us the news we feared would come some day, but still left us in shock: Jeff, my middle son, had been admitted to a hospital in Denver with massive internal bleeding due to AIDS and had only days, if not hours, to live.

Horrified, our minds became totally disheveled as we attempted to respond. For a few moments it was as though we had a complete disconnect from all reality: "Is this really happening? Is this diagnosis from the doctors? Are you sure it's terminal?"

No one knew he had AIDS, not even his family or closest friends.

We soon found ourselves racing to catch the last flight out of Pittsburgh for Denver. By God's providence, ninety minutes later we were sitting in a half-filled Boeing 727, waiting to pull away from the gate for a trip like we had never taken before—and hopefully never will again!

Once airborne, my thoughts raced back to Jeff's youth: his profession of faith in Christ Jesus; his involvement with youth activities at our local church; his intellect and tremendous potential; his position on the high school wrestling team. I also recalled later events in his life, such as his entering Baylor University and being assigned a homosexual roommate, as well as the revelation that his pastor in Waco,

Texas, was a homosexual. I relived that infamous evening of June 30, 1984, when Jeff flaunted his homosexuality in a West Hollywood restaurant and declared, "I never want to see you again." He became so enraged with my position on homosexuality that he changed his last name from Burr to his biological mother's maiden name, since she was sympathetic to his position.

Indeed, it had been a long and agonizing fifteen years since I had last seen Jeffrey, and much carnage had flowed under the bridge of life. Even though our communications had been somewhat restored in the last three years, whenever we scheduled reconciliation visits, he would never show up. Now we found ourselves on a three-and-a-half-hour flight that would eventually bring us face-to-face with this disaffected son.

Having no idea of what we were walking into, my wife Anastasia and I prayed fervently that God would grant us an extra portion of grace, wisdom and strength. We discussed the possibility of taking Jeff back to our home to care for him in his remaining days, should God graciously extend his life. Since Anastasia is a registered nurse, though not his biological mother, she would have the necessary skills for his care at home. But, most significantly, we prayed passionately that the Spirit of the living God would create within my thirty-eight-year-old son the *heart of a little boy* and a *repentant spirit*.

Upon arriving in his hospital room at 11:50 p.m. Denver time, we knew immediately that the Spirit of Christ had preceded our arrival, for Jeff greeted us with tears of joy, saying repeatedly, "Dad, I'm so sorry. . . . I love you, I love you!" We loved on each other as God proceeded to reconcile a father with his estranged son. But this was just the beginning of the most awesome display of God's presence, power and loving-kindness that we have ever witnessed!

Family Background

Perhaps a glimpse of our family background would help you to better understand the events leading up to this emotionally charged reunion.

I was privileged, along with my older brother, to be born to righteous parents who truly modeled love, respect in their marital relationship and an abiding faith in Christ. Our father was a masculine man with a loving heart and a great sense of humor. A banker with enormous integrity, he consistently modeled an impeccable work ethic. Mother was a quiet, gracious and godly woman who superintended our household and gave unsparingly to her family—a "Proverbs 31" type of lady. Never did I hear an argument or see disharmony between my parents, nor was there ever any use of profane language. It was a classic model of a middle-income Christian marriage between two people who feared God and had graciously survived the Great Depression.

In spite of this godly upbringing and my profession of faith at the age of twelve, I took a different course upon entering college. To my shame, this was my entry point into the world, the beginning of my "twenty years of darkness," from age eighteen to thirty-eight. It was during this period that the world encroached upon my fleshly desires and I began "partying" against God. This spawned indulgences in worldly pleasures, a delight in riches and possessions and a thirst for positions, power and applause.

Following college, I entered the military and flew with Strategic Air Command (USAF), where I sunk even deeper into the cesspool of the world, playing it "fast and loose." During the final months of my tour of duty, I became involved with a very free-spirited and attractive airline stewardess. After only a few weekends of courtship—and sadly, in the midst of folly—we came together through the marriage covenant only to marginalize its lifetime commitment and accompanying family values.

From that unpropitious beginning came twins, one of whom was stillborn. The surviving twin, Timothy, was joined a few years later by his younger brothers, Jeffrey and Bruce. Regrettably, though, their father continued in his pursuit of gold and silver, believing that this would give purpose to his life and satisfy the emptiness of his soul.

But by the mercy of God, the eternal Redeemer rescued me when I reluctantly attended a Methodist laymen's retreat in central Florida. I was graciously convicted of my sin and, by God's sovereign grace, I experienced the miracle of the second birth by becoming a new creature in Christ. The new language of Canaan was planted in my soul (replacing my old vocabulary, which could turn the air blue!). All things were new! Our merciful God was faithful to His promise: "I will restore to you the years that the swarming locust has eaten" (Joel 2:25, NKJV). To this very day, I haven't recovered from that divine appointment with God on October 10, 1970!

At the time of my conversion to Christ, the boys were between the ages of nine and thirteen and I was thirty-eight years of age. They now had a new father who attempted to make up for lost ground, but, regrettably, their mother and I were not of like heart, mind and purpose. When our youngest son turned twenty-one, she sought a divorce, dissolving our twenty-six-year marriage and remarrying.

Tragically, it was in this unsettling environment that Jeffrey attempted to find his way into a compromising world that would eventually consume him with its guile.

A Family Reunion

Gathered in Jeff's hospital room that Friday night were his mother with her husband, Jeff's younger brother, Bruce,

Anastasia and I. As I said before, this was the first time in over fifteen years that Jeff and I had seen each other.

Moments after our arrival, the doctors gave us a briefing on Jeffrey's condition: He had been found unconscious in the hallway of his apartment at approximately 1:00 a.m. that Friday due to massive bleeding, and was rushed to the Swedish Medical Center in Denver, where he was given continuous blood transfusions. It was determined that he was in the last stages of Kaposi's sarcoma, a cancer that is common to AIDS patients who do not seek treatment for HIV. It affects both the internal organs and the skin. As a result, purple blotches of various shapes and sizes covered his entire body. His doctors described his small and large intestines as "an old thread-worn tire" that would surely puncture and lead to a painful death should surgery be attempted. He had also contracted pneumonia because of his weakened immune system.

Death was imminent, and the only hope was that transfusions of blood would stabilize his condition, stop the bleeding and possibly give him a few weeks of extended life. If this were to occur then he could be released to a hospice center for his final days.

It was at this point that Anastasia and I looked at each other and almost simultaneously suggested that we would love to take Jeff to our home in western Pennsylvania instead of placing him in a hospice. We'll never forget Jeff's reaction—it was as if he had been hit with a bolt of lightning! He lit up like a Christmas tree and joyously accepted our invitation. His extraordinary response was apparently because he had believed, through Satan's deception, that his father did not love him.

The next day, Saturday, more tests were performed and, to everyone's surprise and joy, about midday, his bleeding did stop. We began to make preparations for taking him home. How would we transport him to Pennsylvania? We would give him our master bedroom on the first floor; we would make arrangements with the local hospice nurses to work alongside Anastasia; we would invite our friends to have times of fellowship with him; we must have parties for him and saturate him with our love. He continued to be stable throughout that day and our hearts were enormously encouraged and hopeful.

The Dreaded News

However, the next morning (Sunday), we were informed that Jeff had started bleeding again during the night. The prospects for his survival looked very grim, but we were assured that everything possible would be done to extend his life. More tests were to be performed that morning.

Early that Sunday afternoon of October 31, when we again met with the medical team, we received the dreaded news we didn't want to hear: "His condition has so deteriorated that he will never leave this hospital and death is imminent." Jeff was then informed of his ominous condition and given his options, none of which held any promise. He elected to terminate all blood products and to receive a sedative and a painkiller, which, without accelerating the dying process, would induce sleep and help him to pass away comfortably.

When Anastasia and I entered his room following this sorrowful news, Jeff greeted us with, "You guys know that I'll never be going back to Pennsylvania, don't you?"

"Yes," we responded, with great effort to hold back our tears. We attempted to play down this *temporal* trip to Pennsylvania by pointing him to the *eternal* trip that would bring him face-to-face with his Creator. I asked if he were ready for this ultimate encounter and he responded, "No, I'm not," but quickly added, "Will you help me, Dad?"

With a heart that was breaking, I responded, "Certainly, son; however, I can only escort you to the throne of grace and

then you're on your own. It will be your heart dealing directly
with the heart of God, but Christ the Mediator will be there—
the One who paid the ransom for your life."

He seemed to understand. Then he asked me to help him
through the process of getting right with his Maker.

With his family gathered around him, Jeff prayed for God's
mercy and forgiveness. His prayer went something like this:

> *Almighty God . . . Lord Jesus, I acknowledge my wicked
> sins and beg for mercy. I repent of my wretched deeds and
> lifestyle. Even though I deserve eternal punishment, I plead
> that You will give me a bath . . . cleanse me with Your pre-
> cious blood and make me pure within. I ask that You would
> extend Your grace to me by becoming my Lord and Savior
> and taking me as Your adopted child for all eternity. And,
> as an act of faith, I wish to express my gratitude by thank-
> ing You for hearing and answering the plea of this repen-
> tant sinner. I pray all of this in Your most powerful name,
> the name of Jesus, who is the risen and living Savior. Amen.*

Victory in Jesus

Before our very eyes we saw the transformation of our
son! There was an immediate change of his disposition that
produced an indescribable peace, childlike faith, joy and absolute fearlessness in the face of death. His mother, who was
very close to him and a witness to all these events, described
it this way: "*He had become like a little boy.*" All of the effemi-
nacy, restlessness, anxiety and vanity that had characterized
much of his life was stripped away! He had experienced his
second birth and was now a *new creature* in Christ!

Following this we read from Revelation, chapters 4 and 5,
depicting what the throne room of heaven would be like. Jeff
responded with such joyful expressions as, "I can't wait to see
the gates of heaven," "It's hard to believe that I'll be in heaven
before you, Dad," and "I can't wait to see Jesus."

He then turned to his mother and asked her to notify his employer, a major airline, of his death. He instructed her about the location of his personal effects, of various people to inform and other particulars. What amazed us was his *total peace* in such horrid circumstances; it was as if he were simply preparing for another usual trip. In reality he was—only this one would take him to his Redeemer for all of eternity!

With his family gathered around him and his favorite meal before him, we held Jeff's memorial service while he was still with us. We shared some precious experiences of the past, we laughed, we prayed and we wept. Finally, he wanted to meet with each one of us privately.

When my turn came, we chatted and stared at each other with smiles and bittersweet tears. My thoughts rushed to Psalm 126:5-6, where the psalmist says, "Those who sow in tears will reap with songs of joy. He who goes out weeping, carrying seed to sow, will return with songs of joy, carrying sheaves with him." My heart was filled with wild swings of emotion. One moment I was overcome with the "what ifs" and the raging thoughts of the wasted years for both of us. The next moment I was overflowing with joy, "for this son of mine was dead and has come to life again; he was lost and has been found" (Luke 15:24, NASB).

We shared some more personal thoughts and then embraced each other, at which point Jeff whispered in my ear words that every father of a prodigal hungers to hear: "You know, Dad, you really are a great man; I love you. . . . I'll see you in a bit."

At 7 p.m. that Sunday, drained of all strength due to the loss of blood, Jeff called his nurse for the injection that would induce sleep leading to his eventual demise. Twenty-six hours later, on Monday, November 1, 1999, our gracious Lord and Savior of life took Jeff home. However, a most extraordinary incident occurred during this time. Just four hours prior to his death, he awoke briefly and greeted those in the room by name, saying, "I love you and I'm waiting for them to come and take me to heaven." Immediately afterward, he slipped back into a coma. We received this as the Lord's final affirmation of Jeff's ultimate destiny.

The ferocious battle for his soul was over. Our sovereign God had won—as He always does—and Satan, that "murderer from the beginning" (John 8:44), was crushed once again in total defeat! Our great and glorious Redeemer had snatched our son from the Destroyer's snare in the very final moments of life, saying in effect, "Satan, you can have this useless and wasted shell of a body, but I am taking the soul of Jeffrey Scott Burr to be My adopted child for all eternity and will give him a new and incorruptible body!" And our own hearts were immensely affirmed with the eternal truth that no sinner can drift so far from his Creator that the redemptive love of Jesus cannot reach him!

Jeff's ultimate destiny has now been fulfilled as requested by Jesus in His high priestly prayer: "Father, I want those you have given me to be with me where I am, and to see my glory" (John 17:24). He is now home in heaven, experiencing the glory promised by Jesus, to which we look forward with great expectancy. In the meantime, we who remain are called to run the race to the very end, knowing that our sovereign Lord "will respond to the prayer[s] of the destitute; he will not despise their plea" (Psalm 102:17) and will draw sinners unto Himself by His *irresistible grace!*

Hallelujah, Thine the glory; hallelujah, amen! By Thy grace, O Lord, we'll see our son again!

TWO

For this son
of mine was dead
and is
alive again,
he was lost
and is found.

Some Cold, Hard Facts

As you have read the story of my son Jeff, it may have brought to mind a question you have probably asked at one time or another: What causes someone to become a prodigal?

It is interesting to note that Jeff followed the same pattern in his spiritual journey to faith as I did: eighteen years with a reputation as a "good boy," including a profession of faith, followed by twenty years of darkness, characterized by a rejection of childhood values, morals and faith, before finally coming to repentance and faith in Jesus Christ. But how can we possibly reconcile those early years of obedience with the later years of self-indulgence and rebellion to the will of God?

To be theologically exact, I can only conclude that it should have been considered *thirty-eight* years of darkness! Even though we both made professions of faith and were perceived as "good boys" during our first eighteen years of life, our behavior thereafter told another story.

Never Truly Repented

In order to begin praying rightly for your prodigal, you need to face a few hard facts. First, as hard as it may be for you to admit it, you need to accept that your prodigal *may* have never come to true faith in Christ, even if he prayed a prayer for salvation or went forward during a meeting. We must realize that *faith not preceded by repentance and not followed by obedience is not New Testament faith.* This will be discussed in greater detail in chapter 7.

Admittedly, this can be a difficult and painful realization, but you should not see it as a necessary reflection upon your parenting skills. Some parents interpret Proverbs 22:6, "Train a child in the way he should go, and when he is old he will not turn from it," as an absolute guarantee that, as long as they train them well, their children will grow up to become model Christians. When their child becomes a prodigal, they blame themselves, asking the guilt-ridden question, "What did I do wrong?"

Tom Allen, in his booklet, *Hope for Hurting Parents*, reminds us that this promise in Proverbs must be balanced against the fact that God will not violate the freedom of choice of our children.

> Even our God, the Father-model for all moms and dads, has had trouble with His chosen children of Israel. He has grieved over His wandering, rebellious offspring since the beginning of time. . . . If the perfect Heavenly Father can be a hurting parent, who are we to judge the spirituality of ourselves or other parents solely by the behavior of a son or daughter?[1]

Giving in to parental guilt like this will only tear you apart inside. There is no one who is blameless. If there is, I have never met that person. And for my own part, I have many regrets. If my boys became prodigals, they certainly had a good teacher, because for the first ten to thirteen years of their lives I lived as a heathen. And even now I am no different than my fellow Christians. We are nothing more than a group of continuously repenting sinners—redeemed by the grace of God. There is not a perfect one of us in the whole bunch.

You Need to Share Your Burden

Another cold, hard fact you must accept is that you cannot carry this burden alone. You need to share the story of your prodigal with other believers and not be ashamed. The devil will work overtime to convince you to keep this pain a deep, dark, private secret. I know, because I did—until a pastor helped me escape from my self-imposed prison of pride.

"Richard," he said to me one day, "why don't you come on Sunday night and share your testimony?" He knew about my son being a homosexual, but I had never shared that publicly—only with him. And as we walked out on the platform that Sunday evening, he turned to me and whispered, "I want to hear the whole testimony." He looked at me and smiled and I knew what he was talking about. I had not prepared for this, but he said he would be praying for me.

So after the preliminaries, the pastor introduced me and I went to the pulpit to share. When I came to the part of my story that included Jeff, I skipped over it; I just mentioned him and moved on. But the Lord brought me under deep conviction for being less than forthright with my weighty burden. It was like the strong arm of God reaching out and pulling me back to that episode. So I went back and shared just enough about his lifestyle to solicit prayer for him. (My pastor friend must have been praying, "Lord, don't let him skip over it!")

I thank God for that experience because that was a point of personal liberation. I remember weeping in the pulpit as I told the story. And as I shared, others in the congregation began to weep as well. I came to realize that they were helping me to bear my burden, as it is taught in Galatians 6:2: "Carry each other's burdens, and in this way you will fulfill the law of Christ." And "the law of Christ" is: "Love one another. As I have loved you, so you must love one another" (John 13:34).

Since that time I have shared Jeff's story many times before other groups. What I discovered was that someone will invariably come up and say, "We have a son or daughter in similar circumstances," while others will come and say, "We have a prodigal, but not quite as bad." But how do you measure the depth of "bad"? Are we not all prodigals? A prodigal is characterized by intemperate and extravagant living, as though he is hastening his own death by digging his own grave. The only question is how far you and I have gone down that road. I empathize with these folks and encourage them to go back to their prayer chambers, because that is the only place where we can find the needed comfort. Yes, we may go in weeping, but invariably we will come out rejoicing!

I have often thought, *If I had never shared that truth, I would never have had the chance to encourage those people or to receive encouragement from them.* It seems that one of the greatest problems in the Christian Church today is our unwillingness to be transparent before others.

Part of the reason for this may be pride[2], parental guilt feelings or simple embarrassment. Probably the greatest cause of this lack of transparency, however, is the absence of deep relationships within congregational life, which is a reflection of the twenty-first-century culture in which we live. Everyone is living at such a fast pace that we have no time for each other. When we come to church, we're in and then quickly out again. We live in a culture where vulnerability is a fearful thing. We can't trust other people, because we don't know them—or perhaps we know them all too well!

Take the time to slow down your life and develop a close friendship with a believer who will listen to and understand you. Once you start to share with others, you will likely find that you are not the only one with a prodigal.

And don't limit your sharing only to the parents of adult children. A child is just one kind of prodigal. All of us have loved ones—whether children, parents, siblings or friends—who are estranged from God. With the passing of years, a sort of "acceptance" sets in. The devil would have us be resigned to the idea that the situation is hopeless. By sharing our burden with others, and praying with them, we receive hope and support.

You Cannot Go after Your Prodigal

Another cold, hard fact is that you cannot go running after your prodigal; he has to come home himself. The old maxim, "A person convinced against his will is of the same opinion still," is true. However, the good news is that the "Hound of the heavenlies" can change a person's will and draw your prodigal home. This is a major function of the Holy Spirit that you should be praying for; we will discuss this in greater detail in chapter 6.

I know of a father who learned this truth the hard way. His son was raised in the Church and at the age of fifteen was introduced to drugs—on a trip with the church youth choir, no less! The parents knew nothing about it until they started to see a decline in their son's grades, along with a change in his personality. He went from being a straight-A student to barely making it through high school.

The father and his wife professed to be believers; they attended a Bible-believing church. However, when the drug use came out in the open, his wife, as it turned out, was sympathetic to the child, which caused a breach in their marriage relationship (prodigals have a way of creating a wedge between husband and wife). As the situation went from bad to worse, the father said, "I felt so lonely, so isolated, that I seriously thought of taking my own life."

A Christian businessman, a family friend in another state, suggested, "Why don't you send your son over to me? I will employ him, get him into the right circles and see that he starts at our community college this fall." Out of desperation, the parents sent their son to him. The plan lasted about four months. The son ran away and was soon back with his old high school friends, doing drugs. In the meantime, the parents had relocated from the West Coast to the East Coast, so that their son was now nineteen and living on the other side of the country, estranged from his parents and in trouble with the law.

Needing some counsel, the father talked to his pastor, who exhorted him to reach out to his son in a more aggressive way. "You have to enter into the arena of his life and literally rescue him."

And that is what he did. At great personal cost, the father traveled by auto across the country to the town in which he used to live. The first thing he did when he arrived in town was to stop at the local barber shop. He asked the barber, "If I wanted to buy some drugs, where would I go?"

The barber replied, "Where all the kids are hanging out—on the beach." The distressed father disguised himself and went out to the beach, praying, "Oh, Lord, direct me to my son." He spent days in fruitless searching. It seemed like there were thousands of kids, all mingling around on the beach.

"I felt as if I was looking for a needle in a haystack," he said. "Finally, after the fourth day I prayed in desperation, 'Lord, I have driven across this entire country; please lead me to him.' No sooner had I put an 'Amen' on that prayer than I looked up and saw my son, standing about a hundred yards away, in a pair of cutoff shorts.

"My heart was pulsating; it felt like it was going to burst through my chest. Now that I had spotted him, I didn't know what to do, because he was among some tough-looking characters. So I moved closer to him, put on my sunglasses, pulled my old sailor's cap down over my head and prayed, 'Lord, please separate him from those other guys.' Suddenly, my son broke away from the others and started walking down the beach by himself."

This was his chance. The father walked up behind his son and slipped his arm up over his shoulder. Startled, the son turned around and his eyes became like saucers. His father was supposed to be on the other side of the country! "What the ____ are you doing here?"

The father responded, "Son, I promised you that I would always come after you because you and I made a covenant—remember? I'm here to take you home."

But it was not to be; this prodigal wasn't ready to go home. After the son regained his composure, he turned to his father in anger and said, "You can take your Christianity and hang it on your beak! I want no part of it!" With that, the father began to weep and attempted to embrace his son, but the son refused.

The father went back to his car and drove home, 3,300 miles cross-country. "During that trip home," he said, "I wept for hours. I had driven for days from coast to coast to find him and he totally rejected me. On the instruction of my pastor I tried to seek him out, but I am now convinced it was the wrong thing to do. Later I studied the story of the prodigal son, and I noticed that the father never went out after the son. He went to the edge of the property, looked out to the horizon and presumably prayed; but he never went into the pigsty!"

Even though in some ways that cross-country trip was a tremendous experience, one that I am sure his son will never forget, this father's attempt to go after his prodigal ended in failure. The son is still apart from his family, in his forties, married with children—and still in the "far country." "I know it will happen in God's time, not mine," the father said recently. "We may not see our prodigal return home on this side of heaven. However, we take great encouragement from Matthew Henry's counsel:

Ordinarily, a vessel retains the savour with which it was first seasoned. Many indeed have departed from the good way in which they were trained up; Solomon himself did so. But early training may be the means of their recovering themselves, as it is supposed Solomon did.[3]

"We are trusting the Father to do for our son what He did for the prodigal in Luke 15!"

How can a man like this continue to trust God for his son after so many years of rebellion? Only by retreating to his secret closet of prayer.[4] He tells me that the only place he finds solace and relief is in solitude with God. "I was never so discouraged in all my life as when I watched my son wither away under the influence of booze and drugs," he said. "That is when I really learned to pray."

It Is Essential to Release Them to God

Just as a pilot needs to maintain a proper altitude to avoid crashing into a mountain, we need to maintain an intimate relationship with Christ to keep from crashing into the circumstances of life. And this brings us to another hard fact we must face: ironically, your overwhelming desire to see your prodigal come home may be one of your greatest stumbling blocks. My son was truly a mountain in my life, and many times I crashed into that mountain until I came to the point where I truly released him to God.

Several years ago, while conducting a conference in a small community church in eastern Connecticut, I found my heart in much need of encouragement. My son had told me he was a homosexual and that he never wanted to see me again. I had just been deserted by my former spouse and was single again, so I was going through this pain alone.

I recall one particular morning on which I was praying through the opening chapters of Revelation. As I prayed through the first chapter, I sensed the comforting work of God's grace. Then I came to the second chapter—Christ's message to the church at Ephesus—and it was there that God truly spoke to me (no, not an audible voice, but the mind of the Spirit ministering to my mind). I will never forget it.

As I came to the second verse, "I know your deeds, your hard work and your perseverance," I remember taking it as God's personal encouragement to this needy soul and responding, "Thank you, Lord, for I am really hurting today."

Continuing on in the same verse, I came to the statement, "I know that you cannot tolerate wicked men." I responded in prayer by saying,

> Lord, of all sins that I abhor, the two greatest are divorce and homosexuality. And now I find myself in the midst of all this! Lord, what is it that You are attempting to teach me?

Then I went on to verse 3: "You have persevered and have endured hardships for my name, and have not grown weary." Now I was somewhat comforted. I said, "Thank you, Lord, for this encouragement. I really needed that."

But then I moved on to verse 4, where it reads: "Yet I hold this against you: You have forsaken your first love." At first I thought this verse didn't apply to me. However, I could sense God saying, *Richard, you've got a problem here.* I will never forget it, because this was a turning point in my spiritual pilgrimage.

At first I started to debate with the Lord. (That is never a good idea, because we always lose!) I reviewed the whole scenario of my prodigal son—all the guilt and everything else that was associated with it—and I said, "Lord, obviously this just doesn't apply to me!" In fact, I tried to move on to the next verse, but the Holy Spirit kept dragging me back to "You have forsaken your first love."

I said, "Lord, You know that I left the business world to go into full-time ministry for You. I live by faith—without any salary; I don't have a pension plan; I don't have all the creature comforts others have; I've even slept in the back of my car, in order to be a good steward of Your provision!"

Richard, I know, the Lord said. *I know all your deeds.*

Continuing, I said, "Lord, I *love* this ministry You have given me!"

And it was when I said, "I *love* this ministry," that He gently spoke to my heart, *Richard, that's the problem. You love the ministry more than you love Me.* Suddenly the issue of my son went off the radar screen. God was now confronting me with the neediness of my own soul.

I came under deep conviction as the Lord took me on to verse 5: "Remember the height from which you have fallen!" Again, I sensed the Lord's instruction: *Richard, I want you to reflect back to when you first gave your heart to Me. Do you remember what those first days were like? Son, I want you to love the Giver of the gift more than you love the gift itself. The issue this morning is not about your son Jeffrey; be assured I'll care for him. But you need to repent and return to your first love, or I will remove your ministry. Yes, you may continue on with your calling, but it will be nothing more than a resounding gong, empty of Me. I want you to love Me with all of your heart, soul, mind and strength.*

That morning I spent several hours on my knees before the Lord in repentance. It was a turning point. My entire soul was redirected as I began focusing on the vertical again. That is, the eyes of my heart became riveted upon God's immutable attributes instead of being fixed upon the circumstances surrounding my life. I became overwhelmed with His majesty, holiness and boundless love, as I had been in those initial days following my conversion. And my heart was gloriously filled with an inexpressible joy, love and assurance that God *would* display the power of His works in the lives of my loved ones. It was as though God was saying, *Richard, you have carried this burden long enough; now be still and remain in My love. Do not fret; trust Me with your son—for My love for Jeffrey is infinite, while yours is imperfect at best.*

Suddenly the weighty burden for my wayward son and the anxiety that had gripped my soul for years was wonderfully lifted as the *peace* of God engulfed my soul. Yes, it was an earthly transaction that carried with it a heavenly explanation!

You see, the devil always wants us to gaze upon the horizontal circumstances of life. But God wants us to maintain that upward look, to gaze upon Him (see Hebrews 12:2) and just occasionally glance at our circumstances. When you are gazing on God, He invariably gives you the strength and peace to handle those glances at your circumstances.

Conversely, when you're gazing at your circumstances, they can literally overwhelm you with discouragement, doubt and despair. But when you are caught up into the awesome wonder of who God is and what He has done, with the eyes of your heart riveted upon Him, He will supernaturally empower you to handle anything around you!

You Must Participate in Your Own Funeral

If the key to triumphant Christian living is to maintain our first love for Christ, then how can this passion be preserved—on a daily basis—without being consumed, once again, with that "mountain" of your life?

The answer lies in the understanding and practice of the Master/servant relationship, the cold, hard fact of dying to self. If you take on the attitude of a servant by voluntarily giving yourself over to the Master, you have no *rights*, *possessions* or *will* of your own. You desire *only* the will of God. The Master, for His part, commits Himself to care, protect and provide for you—His servant.

I like to refer to this as "participating in your own funeral on a daily basis." And this is what Galatians 2:20 is all about: "I have been crucified with Christ and I no longer live, but Christ lives in me. The life I live in the body, I live by faith in the Son of God, who loved me and gave himself for me."

Pastor Alistair Begg paraphrases it this way:

> Jesus gave His life for me,
> so that He could take my life from me,
> in order that He can live His life through me.

That's the crucified life! And that can only happen when we come to the end of our rope and sign over everything to Christ. In other words, it's the *total* surrender of our lives to the care, protection and provision of our Master, which constrains us to pray,

> *Lord, I die to my possessions: bank accounts, home and investment portfolios, etc. I die to my precious family, including my beloved prodigal; I die to my positions in life: personal accomplishments, those little initials before or after my name, etc. I die to my privileges and rights; Lord, I yield complete control of my life and family to You, desiring only what You want for us—to be Your faithful and obedient servant.*

We may still have crisis points in our lives, but we will know how to handle them. When a mountain of problems looms before us, we may crash into it, but we won't waste our sorrows by "living at the crash site." Instead, we can pray with contriteness the following:

> *Praise be to You, O God of grace, the Father of our Lord Jesus Christ. To You belongs all glory, majesty, power and authority—for everything in heaven and earth is Yours.*

As Your surrendered servant, I thank You for giving me this cherished prodigal. You know the depth of my love for him/her. And You know the grievous pain of my heart as I have attempted to parent this gift from You. Yet You also know of my failures as a parent and how I've sadly become a participant in making a hash of this relationship.

Therefore, Lord, I acknowledge my egregious ways and beg for mercy and grace. I ask that You would sovereignly intervene in this relationship by adopting my treasured prodigal as Your child for all eternity. And in the process, take this frail parent of the earth and cause me to become a learner and grow into maturity.

Having no idea of when You are going to resolve this, I thank You by faith, in advance, for how You're going to bring this situation to resolution. In the meantime, grant this servant much grace and patience.

I humbly pray this in the hallowed name of Jesus Christ.

If you have read this far, you may have come to realize that you have your priorities inverted: You have established the return of your prodigal as your primary concern and made God's glory a secondary matter. Remember, the chief reason for which we all have been created is to glorify God, to enjoy Him forever and to love Him with all our heart, soul, mind and strength. But the enemy of our souls will always attempt to invert the primary with the secondary, rendering us helpless in our pursuit of God.

So how do we maintain that passion for Christ? The answer is found in our Lord's teaching in Luke 9:23: "If anyone would come after me, he must deny himself and take up his cross *daily* and follow me." It is not annually at a prayer conference, but *daily*—and that takes us back to our *daily* appointment with God in our secret closet of prayer (Matthew 6:6).

Having dealt with these cold, hard facts, the question then arises—what is the role of prayer in bringing our prodigals home? We will discuss this in the next chapter.

THREE

For this son
of mine was dead
and is
alive again,
he was lost
and is found.

The Role of Prayer

The Necessity of Prayer

Ever since the "homegoing" of Jeffrey, my mind has frequently wrestled with the question, "What will be my greatest surprise when God calls me to my heavenly home?" Of the many thoughts that have rushed through my mind as possible answers to that question, the most awesome has been the reality of being thoroughly emancipated from all temptation, free from my old fleshly nature, and gazing upon the unveiled face of God. To experience the fulfillment of that beatific vision, to "see him as he is" (1 John 3:2), will be the greatest gift one could ever receive, the height of spiritual ecstasy. And to think that it will last for all eternity!

That is my greatest expectation. However, I believe my greatest *surprise* will be the full realization of the stupendous power of prayer to which I had access while on earth—but how infrequently I used it! To realize, from that glorified position, the fruitlessness of my time spent on earth in worrying, frittering away precious time, pursuing worthless strategies and engaging in meaningless rhetoric over issues of no eternal consequence will undoubtedly be shocking.

In his letter to the Philippians, the Apostle Paul encourages us to pray about everything (4:6), to think on things that are positive and holy (4:8) and, finally, to act on what we have learned and seen (4:9). It is not a coincidence that the sequence is "pray-think-act." Paul purposely wrote those verses in that progression, because God intends us to follow that order. All too often we sabotage this process, so that it deteriorates into "act-think" or "think-act"—and when all else fails, then "pray"!

You may recall the story I told in the previous chapter of the father who went out to find his prodigal son. He drove across the country and spent days in fruitless searching—until he prayed. And after God graciously allowed him to find his son, he didn't pray for God to give him the wisdom to say the right thing; instead, he tried in his own wisdom to persuade his son to come home, which he now realizes was the wrong thing to do.

Certainly that is an example of thinking and acting before praying—and you can see how little it accomplished! When we replace the primary ("pray") with the secondary ("think" and "act"), this perilous inversion of Truth itself prevents the divine power of God from making us effective in prayer and in fruit-bearing.

Prayer and God's Word

Jesus spoke to this relationship between prayer and fruit-bearing when delivering His final message to His disciples on the night of His arrest. Knowing that they would be tempted to scatter and possibly return to the Law following His crucifixion, He exhorts them, "I am the vine, you are the branches. He who abides in Me, and I in him, bears much fruit; for *without Me you can do nothing*" (John 15:5, NKJV).

That we believers are the branches of this vine implies that Christ is also the root. This is not just an ordinary root, but a most unique, one-of-a-kind rootstock that produces a sap—that divine power of God (i.e., the Holy Spirit)—which flows through the vine to the grafted-in branches, causing them to flourish and to be fruitful. And carefully superintending this spiritual vineyard is the Father, who has a proprietary interest in the vine and the branches, as well as the fruit.

It is in this context, as the Church is about to be birthed, that Jesus exhorts His disciples to be His "fruit-bearers." Not only were they to display the "fruit of the Spirit" (Galatians 5:22) in their daily living, but they were also expected to be actively involved in the extension of His kingdom on earth (Acts 1:8). They were to be His witnesses—just as we are called to be—in proclaiming the good news to the uttermost parts of the world, thus bearing "much fruit, showing yourselves to be my disciples" (John 15:8).

In order to bring forth this fruit, Jesus lays out the essential requirement of remaining in Him. The disciples were to yield the totality of their lives to Christ, thus forming a constant union with Him that could only be maintained through the means of prayer and the instruction of His Word. Notice how the text reads: "If you remain in me and my words remain in you, ask whatever you wish, and it will be given you. This is to my Father's glory, that you bear much fruit, showing yourselves to be my disciples" (15:7-8). Kenneth S. Wuest has effectively translated this fundamental truth to bring out the richness, force and clarity of the Greek text. Thus, it becomes one of the most compelling and striking commands, along with its promise, to be found in all of Scripture:

> If you maintain a living communion with Me [i.e., *prayer*] and My words [i.e., the *Word* of God] are at home in you, *I command you to ask*, at once, something for yourself, whatever your heart desires, *and it will be yours*. In this My Father is glorified, namely, that you are *bearing much fruit*. So shall you become My disciples.[1]

Notice the profoundness of these verses. It suggests that just as Aaron and the Old Testament high priests were appointed to enter the Holy of Holies and stand boldly before Almighty God, we as New Testament believer-priests have an even greater charge. For we "are a chosen people, a royal priest-

hood" (1 Peter 2:9), having the privilege to "approach God
with freedom and confidence" (Ephesians 3:12). Jesus' statement in John 15:7, "Ask whatever you wish, and it will be
given you," implies that the wealth of God's unsearchable
riches is available to us!

As astounding as it seems, God is actually inviting us to
share in His *creatorship* and *power* by saying, in essence, "I
command you to choose that which you will have . . . and it
will be yours." In other words, He purposes to join with His
"chosen people" as cocreators and coarchitects in building
His kingdom on earth. It was Pascal who asked, "Why has
God established prayer?" And to his own question, he replied, "to communicate to His creatures the dignity of cau-
sality"—or, as Alexander Whyte put it, "to give us a touch
and taste of what it is to be a creator."[2]

Herein lies the secret of praying the prodigal home—and of
explosive church growth. The underlying combination of
God's Word with the ministry of prayer[3] releases the *divine
power* of God to produce unfathomable results. Wayward children are reconciled to God and to their parents; sinners are
brought under conviction; souls are born into the family of
God. These are not just new bodies in the pews or new names
on the church roll through transferred growth, but new *converts*—genuine disciples of Christ—and real growth of the
kingdom of God on earth as well as in heaven. When we pray
according to God's Word, the Spirit of Truth flows through the
Word to govern our minds and structure our prayers in such a
way as to conform to the Master's will. As someone has ob-
served, "The Spirit rides best in His own chariot."

The disciples obviously embraced these truths, for John the
Apostle affirms, "This is the confidence we have in approach-
ing God: that if we ask anything according to his will, he hears
us. And if we know that he hears us—whatever we ask—we

know that we have what we asked of him" (1 John 5:14-15). And again, he declares, "Dear friends, if our hearts do not condemn us [i.e., no unconfessed sin], we have confidence before God and receive from him anything we ask, because we obey his commands and do what pleases him" (3:21-22).

The Source of Such Power

With such extraordinary promises regarding prayer, it is easy to be drawn into worshiping the *means* through which this power flows instead of the One who bestows such power. Tragically, many perceive this divine power as some mystical influence that happens when they recite and repeat rote prayers or perform certain rituals.

On the contrary, this power is literally the divine power of God—the sap of the vine that flows through the branches, producing much fruit. It is the supernatural work of the Holy Spirit. It is the same power that resurrected Jesus from the dead and lifted Him to the Father's side. This is why Jesus commanded His disciples to "wait for the gift my Father promised . . . [for] you will receive power when the Holy Spirit comes on you" (Acts 1:4, 8). The Lord knew they could not possibly be faithful and bear lasting fruit without first being empowered by the "Supercharger" of life—the blessed Holy Spirit.

This same truth applies to us today. When one genuinely repents and anchors his faith in Christ Jesus *alone*—at that very moment of spiritual re-creation—the person of the Holy Spirit comes to take up permanent residence within the new believer's heart (Romans 8:9-11). The Holy Spirit is a divine person who has all the distinguishing characteristics of personality (i.e., mind, emotion, will) and is equal in essence to God the Father and God the Son. He is not an "it," or a ghost, or some vague influence emanating from God—He is God!

Unfortunately, some refer to the Spirit in these terms and think that the power of the Holy Spirit is "something" they can pick up and use, *rather than a Person who wants to use them!* Therefore, as we are emptied of self and yielded to the Spirit of Christ, we will discover that we can pray effectively, live victoriously and bear much fruit. "His divine power has given us *everything* we need for life and godliness" (2 Peter 1:3).

Not only is the Holy Spirit the Spirit of power, but also He is the Spirit of prayer. We are instructed by the prophet Zechariah that God "will pour out on the house of David and the inhabitants of Jerusalem a spirit of grace and supplication" (12:10). Since man is incapable of praying effectively when left to himself, the Spirit of supplication (i.e., the Holy Spirit) comes to the believer's aid by helping him in his feebleness. The Apostle Paul expresses this quite succinctly in his letter to the Romans: "The Spirit helps us in our weakness. We do not know what we ought to pray for [or how], but the Spirit himself intercedes . . . for the saints in accordance with God's will" (Romans 8:26-27).

In other words, there is no true prayer without the enabling power of the Holy Spirit. Do your prayers for your prodigal seem weak and worthless? The Spirit desires to join His strength with our weakness, in order that we may be the recipients of His promise, "The prayer of a righteous man is powerful and effective" (James 5:16).

The Weapon of Prayer

The Apostle Paul also speaks to this issue of "divine power" in His second letter to the church of Corinth. As he comes to the close of his epistle, we find him defending himself against false apostles who tended to measure everything "by the standards of this world" (10:2). For they perceived Paul's Christlike attitude of "meekness and gentleness" (10:1) as signs of weakness. To counter this carnal criticism, Paul responds by implying that dynamic Christian living "in the world" (10:3) can only be waged as one lays aside the "weapons of the world" (10:4; i.e., worldly wisdom, rhetoric and reliance upon personal strength and credentials) and relies exclusively upon the spiritual weaponry provided by God Himself. Notice how he expresses it:

> For though we live in the world, we do not wage war as the world does. The *weapons* we fight with are not the weapons of the world. On the contrary, they have *divine power to demolish strongholds*. We *demolish* arguments and every pretension that sets itself up against the knowledge of God, and we *take captive* every thought to make it obedient to Christ. (2 Corinthians 10:3-5)

What kind of "weapons" are these that have such "divine power" to tear down the bastions of Satan, to open the blinded minds of unbelievers (4:4) and cause them to "come to their senses and escape from the trap of the devil, who has taken them captive to do his will" (2 Timothy 2:26)? They are the God-given resources of prayer and the Word of God (Ephesians 6:17-18). For these two weapons were designed to work most powerfully in tandem, because *prayer without the Word* leads to mysticism and false religion, and *the Word without prayer* leads to legalism and dead orthodoxy.

Power with God

To help us comprehend this power in prayer and boldness before the face of God, it would be beneficial to revisit Psalm 106, where we find the psalmist lamenting over the rebellion and provocations of the Israelites (recorded in Exodus 32). Tucked away in the middle of this narrative we find a most startling nugget of truth, where the writer declares in Psalm 106:19-21, 23,

> [The Israelites] made a calf
>   and worshiped an idol cast from metal.
> They exchanged their Glory
>   for an image of a bull. . . .
> They forgot the God who saved them,
>   who had done great things in Egypt. . . .
> So he said *he would destroy them*—
>   had not Moses, his chosen one,
> *stood in the breach* before him
>   to keep his wrath from destroying them.

Take careful notice of that last phrase: "had not Moses, his chosen one, stood in the breach before him." This implies that Moses had an inveterate burden and a holy boldness to stand before Almighty God and become an advocate for a provoking people. This, of course, is what intercessory prayer is: *interposing before our most gracious God by pleading for His mercy to be dispensed upon a third party.* In return, God accepts our prayers as a means through which He operates and we graciously share in the blessings He bestows upon others!

Now, look at the results of such bold praying: "[It kept] His wrath from destroying them." God mercifully responded to the fervent pleas of Moses for those mutinous Israelites: "Then the LORD relented and did not bring on his people the disaster he had threatened" (Exodus 32:14). Instead of annihilating them, He extended His mercy in response to the passionate prayers of His chosen one, Moses. Can the prayers of one person possibly turn the events for an entire nation? Yes, for this is what literally happened!

Is it possible for believers today to have such influence with God as His "chosen one," Moses, did? Can we "stand in the breach" for our prodigal? Absolutely! His promises are true and His attributes of love, mercy and grace have been extended to us, "a chosen people, a royal priesthood, a holy nation, a people belonging to God" through Jesus Christ (1 Peter 2:9). This truth is affirmed by one of Christendom's greatest expositors, the eminent Matthew Henry, who said, "God not only pardons upon the repentance of sinners, but He also spares and reprieves upon the intercession of others for them."[4]

By using His commands, invitations and promises as our basis of authority, we can pray His favor upon those who deserve His condemnation—including our prodigals. Don't forget His promise in John 15:7: "If you remain in me and my words remain in you, ask whatever you wish, and it will be given you."

Power with Man

Not only do we have power with God in prayer, but we also have power with man and power against the world system as we seek to declare the glory of God and to reach lost souls. A classic example of God unleashing His divine power to thwart human plans is found in Acts 12, the signature chapter for power intercession, where the newly founded church in Jerusalem comes under heavy persecution by wicked King Herod.

After putting James to death, Herod has Peter thrown into a high-security prison to await a similar fate. However, Luke, the writer of Acts, adds this short statement, seemingly as a hint to what is about to happen: "but the church was earnestly praying to God for him" (12:5).

The night before Peter's trial, as he sleeps chained between two guards and surrounded by sixteen soldiers, a brilliant "light shone in the cell" (12:7). The power of God travels like a laser beam as the apostle is awakened with a voice saying, "Quick, get up!" Suddenly the chains fall off his wrists and he is escorted to freedom by an angel of the Lord. They rush past two guards without being noticed and come to an iron gate that leads to the city, which miraculously opens by itself. It is only when Peter gets out into the street that he comes to his senses and realizes that he is not dreaming; he has been truly rescued by the sovereign power of God.

Moments later the apostle arrives at the house of John Mark's mother—and what do you think they are doing? It says that "many people had gathered and were praying" (12:12). This act of concerted and united prayer—without ceasing—in concert with the grace of God, was the means through which God unleashed His power and provided Peter's supernatural deliverance from certain death.

These first-century Christians were not only living out what Jesus had commanded them to do, "at all times to be praying and not to be losing courage,"[5] but they were also the recipients of what He had promised: "I tell you the truth, if you have faith as small as a mustard seed, you can say to this mountain, 'Move from here to there' and it will move. *Nothing will be impossible for you.* But this . . . does not [happen] except by *prayer and fasting*" (Matthew 17:20-21).

These believers learned that, in such adverse circumstances, their most effective recourse—indeed, their only recourse—was the prevailing power of prayer, not only for the fight against their enemies, but more importantly for the bestowing of God's favor upon His "chosen ones" and for the extension of Christ's kingdom on earth.

The same is true for us today. The only recourse we have against the hold of this world on our prodigal is the prevailing power of prayer. For in reality, the case of Peter also illustrates the condition of our rebellious loved ones and other unbelievers. They are chained by their sin and unable to escape. They're even asleep and insensitive to their plight and destined to die in it—*unless* released by some external power. As it was with the group of believers gathered at Mary's house in Jerusalem, so it is with us today; God has ordained intercessory prayer as a means through which He graciously unleashes His transcendent power to loosen chains and set the captives free.

The eminent expositor, Martyn Lloyd-Jones (1899-1981), while preaching on this passage expressed it this way:

> It matters not what your situation may be, however dark, however black, however tight your bonds, however imprisoned and fettered you may be; if God wills your deliverance, it can be done, it will be done! Prison cells, and wards, and chains and iron gates—they are nothing to God who made the world and sustains everything by His power.[6]

Definition

With these foundational truths of intercessory prayer in mind, we now come to the specific issue of interceding for unbelievers. With the earlier definition of intercessory prayer in view, we can now draw down a more exact definition of praying for lost souls:

> It is the affectionate and persistent outreach of one's heart toward God, that He—by His mercy and grace—may so release His convicting power upon a sinner that the sinner would find it easier to *yield* to the *compelling tug* of the Holy Spirit than to continue in his native rebellion.

A firm belief in this truth—that we are privileged to join with the most Sovereign through prayer and His Word—is foundational and essential in praying for our prodigals and seeing the transformation of sinners. If this is truly our conviction, then we will persevere in it and by God's grace "bear much fruit, showing [ourselves] to be [His] disciples" (John 15:8). In fact, the reality of this truth, along with the principles that are about to be unfolded, becomes the launch pad through which dynamic evangelism is established and sustained.

FOUR

For this son
of mine was dead
and is
alive again,
he was lost
and is found.

God Desires All to Be Saved

From the time I realized that Jeff was a mere *professor of a religion* and not a *genuine disciple of Christ,* I prayed fervently that God our Savior would be merciful in rescuing him from his world of darkness. However, in the midst of those turbulent days I would frequently find my heart being conflicted with fractious emotions. One moment there would be humiliation, the next fury, then guilt and inevitably a deep sense of failure. I refer to this disturbing period of my life as "living at the crash site."

"Mountains" in Our Lives

Since I used to fly in the military, I find myself constantly using military jargon. Therefore, as mentioned in chapter 2, we can look at our Christian life much as a pilot flying a plane. We need to maintain the intimacy of our vertical relationship with God, just as a pilot needs to maintain a proper altitude, or we will crash into a mountain. A "mountain" can be sin, problems, the cares of this world, tribulations, sickness, whatever—anything that threatens to hinder you from being and doing what God would have you to be and do. Furthermore, a "mountain" in your life could be even something "good" that you just don't have in balance.

When we crash into a mountain, we can respond in one of two ways: we can pick ourselves up, dust ourselves off and move on, reestablishing and maintaining that intimate relationship with our Lord; or, we can dwell on the problem—what I call "living at the crash site."

I recently received a letter from a woman I met at one of our conferences. She is a young mother of three children and a very godly, spiritual woman. "I want to ask for prayer," she wrote. "You see, I have my own prodigal now—not my children, but my husband. About a year ago, he told me he was no longer going to live his life to please everyone else. He turned his back on God and told me he didn't love me anymore and that he was leaving the kids and me. He is leading a rebellious life, believing so many lies of the enemy."

She told me that literally hundreds of people were praying for her and encouraging her on a daily basis. Many people are amazed at the peace she has in her life, and she always points them to the Giver of peace. How did she attain this life of victory?

"One of the turning points in all of this for me was on that Tuesday night of the prayer conference, when you were teaching on the 'mountains' in our lives," she wrote. "I didn't realize how much I had been 'living at the crash site.' I have 'crashed' many times since then, but by God's grace, I do not live there. The Lord has given me many passages of Scripture to cling to and to pray through. I am engaged in Scripture praying, and as the result of your teaching, His Word has become my complete sustenance."

Scripture Praying

In coming to terms with my own prodigal, I have much the same testimony as this young woman. Once I embraced the practice of praying Scripture, the Spirit of Christ began to do a new and deeper work within my soul. I started spending protracted periods of time in my "closet of prayer," praying through the Word for a daily cleansing of my soul. Over time I began to sense the healing of my heart, the strengthening of my faith and finally the renewing of my mind with a positive expectation as to *how* and *when* Christ would bring this prodigal son to faith. My whole perspective on the situation changed. The issue was no longer Jeff's homosexuality. The real issue was that *he was a lost soul*—irrespective of his life-style!

By using this practice of praying through Scripture, I was graciously led by the Spirit to the Apostle Paul's teaching to young Timothy (1 Timothy 1:15-2:4). This passage gave me great hope for my son's rebirth, because here Paul lays out his treatise concerning salvation for sinners. With concise-ness and clarity, he gives (1) the purpose of Christ's coming into this world, (2) our Lord's excellencies toward sinners, (3) Paul's own personal wretchedness and (4) the urgency for prayer. Then he concludes with that auspicious pro-nouncement, "God our Savior . . . wants all men to be saved" (2:3-4). On reading this, my heart pounded with excitement as I saw a new hope for my son!

The Purpose of Jesus' Coming

After giving young Timothy a "heads up" as to the impor-tance and worth of what he is about to teach, the Apostle succinctly and profoundly wraps up the entire gospel mes-sage in just nine words: "Christ Jesus came into the world to save sinners" (1:15).

What simplicity! What encouraging news!

But why would the Son of God come from a world of high-est purity into a world of base impurity? The answer is found in the immutable excellency of His unfailing love: "For God so loved the world that he gave his one and only Son, that whoever believes in him shall not perish but have eternal life. For God did not send his Son into the world to condemn the world, but to save the world through him" (John 3:16-17). In essence, it was sinners that drew Him to this planet, for He longed to save them from their depravity and make them as pure as the heaven from which He came!

Therefore, our first appeal in praying for lost souls must always be on the basis of Jesus Christ's sacrificial death for sinners. As Peter proclaimed before the Sanhedrin, "Salvation is found in no one else, for there is no other name under heaven given to men by which we must be saved" (Acts 4:12). We can say with absolute certainty that salvation for all sinners can *only* be found in and through the person of Christ Jesus!

Appealing to His Excellency of Mercy

With this truth fixed in our minds, that Jesus came to salvage sinners, we then appeal for God's *mercy* to be extended to that lost soul for whom we are praying. Paul now explains why he himself was shown such *mercy* in First Timothy 1:16: "But for that very reason I was shown mercy. . . ."

This term *mercy* presupposes sin and infers that God has a "ready inclination to relieve the misery of fallen creatures,"[1] even though they are so undeserving of it. Isn't it interesting that God bestows such favor upon the most unlikely of characters? Paul (formerly Saul of Tarsus), for example, had a "rap sheet" that would have made him a candidate for the TV show *America's Most Wanted.*

Notice how Paul describes his wicked activities prior to his conversion: "I persecuted the followers of this Way to their death, arresting both men and women and throwing them into prison" (Acts 22:4); "I went from one synagogue to another to imprison and beat those who believe in you" (22:19); "I put many of the saints in prison, and when they were put to death, I cast my vote against them. . . . I tried to force them to blaspheme. . . . I even went to foreign cities to persecute them" (26:10-11). He appropriately refers to himself as "a blasphemer and a persecutor and a violent man" (1 Timothy 1:13).

Now, if this picture of Paul's life doesn't "turn your crank" and give you a new hope for that lost soul you've been praying for, then you need a heart transplant! For the greatness of one's sin is no barrier to the extension of God's mercy. It shouldn't be surprising then to see our Lord extend His mercy to Saul—or for that matter, to any of us. "The Lord our God is merciful and forgiving, even though we have rebelled against Him" (Daniel 9:9). One commentator summed it up this way: "Saul, the ultimate sinner, had become Paul, the ultimate saint; God's greatest enemy became His finest servant, and somewhere in between these two extremes fall all the rest of us."[2]

Appealing to His Excellency of Patience

Paul now proceeds to give another reason for being shown such mercy in the second half of First Timothy 1:16: "so that in me, the worst of sinners, Christ Jesus might display his *unlimited patience* as an example for those who would believe on him."

This attribute of God's *patience* (i.e., long-suffering, slowness to anger) is similar to His *mercy*, but with this distinct difference: His *patience* is "that power of control . . . self-restraint . . . that God exercises over Himself"[3] whereby He bears with unbelievers and believers alike. Conversely, His *mercy* rests wholly upon that person to whom He extends mercy: "I will have mercy on whom I will have mercy, and I will have compassion on whom I will have compassion" (Exodus 33:19).

Thus, we have Paul as an example to illustrate our Lord's long-suffering toward us sinners. Instead of Christ drawing the sword of extermination to wipe out this rebel, He treats him magnanimously as though he were a friendly foe. And just at the right time, our Lord drops Saul to his knees through the irresistible Light of Heaven, saying, "Saul, Saul, why do you persecute me?" (Acts 9:4).

Throughout the Bible, and to this present moment, we see the infinite patience of Jehovah in dealing with sinners.

With Israel, He suffered their grumbling and ungratefulness for forty years as they wandered in the desert; thirty-some years with Saul (i.e., Paul); thirty-eight years with my son and me; *one hundred years* with my wife's grandfather (I'll share that story in another chapter)—and look how long-suffering He's been with you!

Why does He extend such patience? He does it to offer more time to bring to Himself His own people, many of whom are not as yet converted! The Apostle Peter affirms this to the brethren as he declares, "He is patient with you, not wanting anyone to perish, but everyone to come to repentance" (2 Peter 3:9).

And those of us who are already in a state of grace and favor with God are to continue growing in His knowledge and holiness and abounding in good works, one of which is praying unceasingly for the extension of His kingdom on earth, including intercession for sinners to come to repentance.

The Urgency of Prayer

With these foundational truths established, Paul now implores young Timothy to integrate prayer with his evangelistic endeavors. Notice the appeal: "I urge, then, first of all, that requests, prayers, intercession and thanksgiving be made for everyone" (1 Timothy 2:1).

Notice carefully the priority that Paul places on praying for others: "*first* of all. . . ." Why such urgency for others? Because it deals with their eternal destiny! And in the Master's economy, He desires to join with the Church in bringing sinners to Himself. Such activity is never wasted time, for "he rewards those who earnestly seek him" (Hebrews 11:6).

Psalm 102:17 says that God "will respond to the prayer of the destitute; he will not despise their plea." The Hebrew word for *destitute* means "to strip oneself." It means to be naked before God. That is just the way I felt with Jeff—like I was stripped of everything. And when I read this verse, I said, "Lord, I am destitute. I am hurting so much I can only go one place and that is up. I know You will not despise my plea. For You do hear the cry of the hurting, the weak, the weary and the wounded."

Sadly, this is what is lacking in much of the Church today—passionate prayer that cries out to God for lost souls. This could be the primary reason why so many churches are experiencing such a drought in genuine conversions. When prayer is meager, invariably it can be traced to the fact that it is *supplemental* rather than *foundational* and *fundamental* to the ministry of the church.

Therefore, in dealing with unbelievers, before we ever approach them with the gospel, we must go to the highest court of appeal. It is here that we have a heavenly Advocate who speaks in their defense to the Judge of all the earth. It is in this court that sinners are set free, for our Advocate Himself has become "the atoning sacrifice . . . not only for our [sins] but also for the sins of the whole world" (1 John 2:2). And we believers have the God-given privilege of appealing to this ultimate Judge, through our Lord Jesus Christ, on behalf of lost souls!

God Wants All to Be Saved

Paul now reaches the summit of his treatise on the salvation of sinners by stating, "God our Savior . . . desires all men to be saved and to come to the knowledge of the truth" (1 Timothy 2:3-4, NKJV). Though sinners deserve to be punished, God would rather see them turn from sin and come to faith in Him. "For I take no pleasure in the death of anyone, declares the Sovereign LORD. Repent and live!" (Ezekiel 18:32).

But we do know that not "all" come to Christ. Why? First, it is important to note that "all" is not a universalistic statement, but refers to the representation of every tongue, tribe and nation. Second, when Scripture states that God "wants all men to be saved" (1 Timothy 2:4) and "[does not want] anyone to perish" (2 Peter 3:9), these are not edicts. They merely express God's *desires* and *wishes,* but not necessarily His sovereign *will.* Otherwise "all" *would* be saved. Third, even though God's salvation is sufficient for the entire human race, Scripture teaches in Romans 3 that all of humanity, Jews and Gentiles alike, are hopelessly separated from God because of their depravity. Therefore, man is incapable of freeing himself from this bondage, and in fact, being so blinded to his situation, he has no desire to even do so.

This condition is graphically illustrated in the life of G. Gordon Liddy, the former White House aide involved in the Watergate scandal. In his autobiography entitled *Will,* Liddy recounts how, while still in prison, he received a visit from the notable Chuck Colson. "Chuck asked me if I had 'seen the light.' 'No,' I replied. 'I'm not even looking for the switch.' " By the way, Liddy is the same fellow who, when asked by David Letterman, "What happens after we die?" responded in his own inimitable way: "We're food for worms." However, after much intercession on the part of friends and exposure to the gospel, Liddy came to the realization that "Christ was who He claimed to be, and he became a Christian."[4]

Left to himself, no man will ever come to Christ. Scripture teaches "there is . . . no one who seeks God. All have turned away, they have together become worthless; there is no one who does good, not even one" (Romans 3:11-12). But as in the life of the Apostle Paul and millions upon millions of others, our sovereign and most merciful God actively intervenes in the lives of His own in such a way as to make certain that they will come to faith.

Since believers have absolutely no idea "on whom He will have mercy," we must make every effort to be actively engaged in the spreading of the gospel and fulfilling the Great Commission (Matthew 28:19-20). Our evangelistic efforts actually become the ordained means through which God brings His own unto Himself.

The bottom line is this: *Our sovereign Lord will never turn away anyone who comes to Him in repentance, trust and faith!*

How Then Should We Pray?

In summary, we have the assurance—from the Author of the Book—that it is His *desire*, His *wish* that everyone would come to repentance. Therefore, with this great expectation in mind, we approach our omnipotent God, asking Him to be glorified through the turning of His *wish* into His *will* for the person for whom we are praying, always being mindful of that previously mentioned promise from our Savior:

> If you maintain a living communion with Me [i.e., prayer] and My words [i.e., the Word of God] are at home in you, *I command you to ask*, at once, something for yourself, whatever your heart desires, *and it will be yours*. In this My Father is glorified, namely, that you are *bearing* much fruit. (John 15:7-8, Wuest)

In praying for Jeffrey, only the Lord knows the number of times I pleaded from the above Scripture for His mercy to be extended to this prodigal. I prayed something similar to the following:

> *Father God—the Creator who gives life to all through the Lord Jesus, the One who came to save wretched sinners such as Paul and multitudes of others including myself—I beg that You would graciously turn Your "wish" into Your*

"will" by allowing Your favor to rest upon my son, Jeffrey Scott Burr.

I plead that You would be merciful and continue to be patient toward Him, for surely he doesn't know what he is doing. Furthermore, You have said that You want "everyone to come to repentance" (2 Peter 3:9). And Lord, I remind You, with much humility and reverence, that You are the Author of this statement.

Therefore, by faith and expectation, I thank you in advance for that day in which You'll bring glory to Yourself by saving my son! Lord, could that day be today? For I pray all of this in the most merciful name of Jesus Christ! Amen.

You may possibly want to pause, ponder and pray for your own prodigal in a similar way. If you wish, use the above model by inserting your prodigal's name and making any other changes you like. Be assured, our precious Savior will hear the cry of your heart!

FIVE

For this son
of mine was dead
and is
alive again,
he was lost
and is found.

The Convicting Power
of the Holy Spirit

uring Holy Week of 1970, I found myself caught in the political crossfire of the corporate world that led to my termination as vice president of a financial services company. The president, a persuasive and shrewd fellow, had found out that I was planning to leave and take a more lucrative position with the parent organization, so he outmaneuvered me by terminating my services before I could resign.

This was of no real concern to me, for I knew I had secured the position for which I was being recruited. However, the next morning I contacted the home office and discovered that I had been "back-doored" by my so-called friend. Since he couldn't censure me for job performance, he implied to them that I had a drinking problem. And because of his political clout with the right people in high places, this fellow Burr was suddenly on the outside looking in. I found myself living in the cold country of northern Wisconsin, with a wife and three young boys, a mortgage and no job. I was devastated!

Fortunately, in the weeks that followed I found other employment and our family relocated to sunny South Florida. In the midst of this whole scenario my soul became noticeably restless and sensitive to the kind of life I was living. I came to a new awareness that I was willfully violating much of what my parents had stood for and taught me. And woven throughout all of this was a deep sense of failure in the various duties and responsibilities of my life.

Being unable to clearly define the cause of such distress, and not wanting anyone to know my dilemma, I decided to attend church—alone. I can't remember much of what was said from the pulpit, but the singing of the old hymns of my youth would move me to tears. Embarrassed by such emotions, I would leave the services early to avoid greeting anyone, particularly the minister. After driving around in my car until the redness of my eyes had cleared, I would then return home feeling worse than when I left. I couldn't understand what was happening. Quite honestly, I thought I was losing my mind!

After several weeks of attending that church, I was invited to attend a men's retreat in central Florida. Though I had absolutely no desire to attend this conference, I reluctantly succumbed to the invitation for some unknown reason.[1] The first evening's speaker was Bill Bright, the founder of Campus Crusade for Christ, talking about the uniqueness of Christ's love as found in First John 1:9: "If we confess our sins, he is faithful and just and will forgive us our sins and purify us from all unrighteousness." (Apparently, Dr. Bright thought he was speaking to a group of Christians since this passage is for believers, not necessarily unbelievers such as I was.)

After his lengthy discourse, he directed us to go off to a solitary place and write down all our sins. I couldn't believe what I was hearing. Asking 500 businessmen to go off and write down their sins? Get real!

I turned to my friend, Walt Perkins, who was a captain with Eastern Airlines, and said, "Hey buddy, I don't know about you, but thirty minutes ain't gonna cover it for me!" He responded, "Yeah, and I'll need a ream of paper!" With that we both laughed and made a mockery of such a request as they passed out paper and pencils to facilitate the exercise.

Moments later, I found myself sitting on the floor in a corner of the dining hall with pencil and paper in hand. Inextricably, through a power which I had never known before, my mind gravitated to the sins of my past. It was as if I were watching that old TV show, *This Is Your Life*—only this time, *I* was the central character! The sins of my life were paraded before the eyes of my heart and, suddenly, it was no longer a joking matter. I felt repulsed by what I was seeing. Instinctively, I began to write down everything that came before my mind. I wrote on both sides of the paper until every square inch was filled. I remember completing the assignment by writing across the bottom of the page, in large, bold letters, "PEACE and PURPOSE." This was what I was truly searching for—a *purpose* for living and *peace* within my soul.

It wasn't until after my conversion that I came to realize that these events, and others, had been graciously orchestrated by the Savior through the activity of the blessed Holy Spirit. I wasn't losing my mind, after all; God was simply sensitizing my heart and preparing me to come to repentance and personal faith in Christ.

The Convicting Power of the Holy Spirit

What I had experienced, like every true convert, was the *convicting power of the Holy Spirit*—that awesome power of God that overwhelms the soul and brings one to his knees. Or, to express it in a more definitive way, it is *the irresistible power of God descending upon one's soul with such magnitude that it not only tears down the strongholds of unbelief and depravity, but also creates within one's heart a state of utter helplessness.*

It is this *convicting power* of the Spirit that is His *initial* work in bringing sinners to salvation in Christ Jesus. The Lord foretells of this work of the Spirit in John's Gospel: "When he [the Holy Spirit] comes, he will convict [i.e., convince, reprove] the world of guilt in regard to sin and righteousness and judgment: in regard to sin, because men do not believe in me" (16:8-9).

The verb *convict* carries with it two basic meanings. One is "to *reprove*," as in calling one's attention to "an error previously held or a wrong previously committed."[2] The other meaning is "to *convince*," for the idea here is "to convince one of some truth previously unknown or unrealized."[3] It is this latter meaning that is appropriate for the context of these verses. It is impossible for man to know the depth and understand the consequences of his sin, much less to respond to the gospel, unless God first *convinces* and then *draws* him.

This work of the Spirit is not just to inform sinners of their folly, but to (1) break down their indifference toward sin, (2) show them that true righteousness can only be found in Jesus Christ and (3) persuade them that judgment is coming, as proved by Satan's condemnation at the cross. Therefore, this all-powerful work of the Spirit is to thoroughly *convince* sinners of

a. the *fact* of sin: showing specifically their act of sin.
b. the *fault* of sin: showing how they are wrong or guilty.
c. the *folly* of sin: showing the foolishness, lewdness and wickedness of their behavior.
d. the *filth* of sin: showing how repugnant sin is to God.
e. the *fountain* of sin: showing the depravity of their souls.
f. the *fruit* of sin: showing that the end thereof is eternal damnation, if they are not regenerated.[4]

Even though it was Dr. Bright who opened the Word and kindly presented the case for Christ at that men's retreat, it was the convicting work of the Spirit that opened my heart. God uses His messengers as reprovers, or heralds of truth, but it is exclusively the Spirit of Truth who convicts and convinces the sinner—prodigal—of his sin.

This truth is clearly illustrated in Acts, where we find the effects of the outpouring of the Holy Spirit upon the 120 believers at Pentecost (Acts 2:1-13). First we find the Apostle Peter, freshly filled with this newfound power of the Spirit, along with the other Eleven, standing and fearlessly proclaiming the most dynamic and divinely inspired sermon ever given on this side of the Resurrection (2:14-36).

Second, we witness the Spirit descending upon the unregenerate hearers with this gospel message, some of whom had nailed Jesus to the cross only weeks prior to this incident. Notice how they responded with a deep sense of helplessness: "When the people heard this, they were *cut to the heart* and said to Peter and the other apostles, 'Brothers, *what shall we do?*' " (2:37).

Upon first reading this Scripture, one could easily be inclined to think that Peter, the fisherman, must have been a most accomplished and eloquent speaker. But in reality, it was the Spirit of Truth who so powerfully gripped the heart of this apostle, who only fifty days earlier had denied even knowing Christ. Now, he was being used as a herald of the gospel and his message traveled like a laser beam to the hearts of his hearers, *cutting* and *piercing* as it went.

Again, this "cutting, piercing, pricking or stinging" is the work of the Holy Spirit as He *convicts* and *convinces* the listeners. For this *cutting* created within their hearts a poignant sorrow, alarm, acknowledgment of their sinfulness and a deep sense of helplessness that caused them to cry out, "Brothers, what shall we do?" To which Peter responded, "Repent and be baptized [i.e., believe], every one of you . . . for the forgiveness of your sins" (Acts 2:38). That day 3,000 new converts were added to the Church!

Why is there so little display of such power today? It is because this *convicting power* of the "Hound of the heavenlies" is missing in much of our evangelism. And when this *convincing* work of the Spirit is absent, genuine faith will never follow! The Barna Survey of Religion in America has stated that slightly more than fifty percent of those who make "decisions for Christ drop out of church participation within six to eight months." The reason for this is that they were never *convicted* and *convinced* of their sin in the first place. And when there is no *conviction of sin* there is no true conversion because there is no sense of one's need for a Savior.

These so-called "decisions for Christ" were actually spurious, because their professions of faith never materialized into any spiritual fruit. The "walk" of their lives didn't match up to their "talk." Tragically, this scene has been repeated endlessly throughout the Church in recent decades, weakening local assemblies and producing mere *professors* of a religion instead of *genuine disciples of Christ*. This was expressly the case with both Jeff and me when we made those professions of faith at the age of twelve.

The renowned R.A. Torrey tells of this issue in his book, *The Person and Work of the Holy Spirit*.[5] Torrey was approached by one of his church leaders, who declared, "I am greatly troubled by the fact that we have so little conviction of sin in our meetings. While we are having many accessions to the church, there is no deep conviction of sin. I propose that we officers of the church meet from night to night to pray that there may be more conviction of sin in our meetings." The leaders began to intercede, and shortly thereafter they experienced the fruit of their praying.

As Torrey was preaching one Sunday evening, he noticed a man leaning further and further forward in his seat. As Torrey tells it,

> In the midst of my sermon, without any intention of giving an invitation, simply wishing to drive a point home, I

said, 'Who will accept Jesus Christ tonight?' Quick as a
flash this man sprang to his feet and shouted, 'I will!' It
rang through the building like the crack of a revolver. I
dropped my sermon and instantly gave out the invitation;
men and women and young people rose all over the
building to yield themselves to Christ. God was answer-
ing *prayer* and the Holy Spirit was *convincing* men of sin!"

What, then, must we do? We must earnestly pray for unbelievers! While the Holy Spirit *convinces* men and women
of sin, He does it by working through *us*—not only as we
witness, but also as we *pray* for lost souls. "Every conversion
recorded in the Acts of the Apostles was through the agency
of men and women already saved."[6]

Ironically, if you search the Scriptures for examples of
how to pray for the lost, you will quickly discover that there
are very few indeed. However, Psalm 83 does give us an il-
lustration of how the psalmist prayed concerning the enemies of God—the foes of Israel. The phrase "enemies of
God" may sound rather harsh, but we should remember that
Jesus declared, "He who is not with me is against me, and he
who does not gather with me scatters" (Matthew 12:30). Ei-
ther you are "in" Christ or "outside of" Christ, a "friend" of
Messiah or a "foe"; there is no middle ground!

The psalmist begins by pleading with God to refrain from
His silence and speak against His foes. He understood that
God's speaking is His acting, for with God, saying and doing
is the same thing. The psalmist then gives an account of
these unregenerate people (83:2-12) that leads up to this
model prayer in verses 13-16 and 18:

> Make them like tumbleweed, O my God,
>   like chaff before the wind.
> As fire consumes the forest
>   or a flame sets the mountains ablaze,
> so pursue them with your tempest

and terrify them with your storm.
Cover their faces with shame
  so that men will seek your name, O LORD. . . .
Let them know that you, whose name is the LORD—
  that *you alone are the Most High over all the earth.*

With these verses in view, and as we intercede for unbelievers, it behooves us to yield to the Spirit by allowing Him to guide our thoughts and shape our supplication. For example, the following prayer is similar to how I prayed for Jeff during those years of his rebellion:

> *Almighty God, the Father of our Lord Jesus Christ, I beg that You, through the Spirit, would pursue and convict my son, Jeffrey.*
>
> *As fire consumes the forest or a flame sets a mountain ablaze, I ask that the heat of the Spirit would create a meltdown within his heart. As the force of a mighty hurricane sweeps across the Atlantic, likewise, would You not graciously put Your loving pressure on him by convincing him of his sins and of Your coming judgment?*
>
> *Give him no rest in his worldly pursuits. Cover his heart and his head with shame because of his sins; create within him an utter helplessness in order that he may become a seeker of You, for "You, LORD, have never forsaken those who seek you" (Psalm 9:10).*
>
> *And magnify Your name by such convicting power that he would come to realize without reservation that You are the Most High over all the earth, and that Jesus Christ, alone, offers him salvation full and free.*
>
> *O God, do whatever is necessary to bring him to repentance and faith in Your Son! It is in the powerful name of the Lord Jesus Christ that I pray. Amen.*

You may ask, "How could you have possibly prayed such a prayer for your son? Did you not love him? Were you not fearful of what God might do to him?"

Yes, I was fearful of what could possibly happen to him, but I was much *more* fearful of his never coming to repentance and faith and being separated from God for all eternity. I loved him deeply. However, my love is imperfect at best. But God's love is absolutely perfect as He draws sinners unto Himself! I was convinced that God loved Jeff much more than I did, and it was this trust that enabled me to ask the Sovereign One to do whatever was necessary to bring my son to Christ. And by His sovereign power, He did just that!

One final thought: Eight months prior to Jeff's death, he went to a dentist to have some dental work done. In the course of the examination the dentist counseled him, "Son, you have no dental problem. I suggest that you go to AIDS Anonymous to be tested." Jeff did and discovered he had HIV. When he told us of this incident on his deathbed, we asked why he had not sought medical treatment, and his reply was, "I was too ashamed!"

Could this have been the softening and convicting work of the Holy Spirit in preparing Jeff for his divine appointment with the Great Mediator? I tend to believe so. I only wish we could have had more time together, for there are many unanswered questions. Even so, it is well with my soul—God is sovereign!

For this son

of mine was dead

and is

alive again,

he was lost

and is found.

SIX

The Drawing of the Spirit

ot only does the *convincing* power of the Spirit of Christ descend upon the soul with such magnitude as to create an utter helplessness within, but also, the Spirit literally *draws* sinners unto the Savior. This truth was gloriously illustrated in my own life when I was invited to that men's retreat back in October of 1970. You may recall that in the previous chapter I mentioned that I had absolutely no desire to attend this conference, but reluctantly succumbed to the invitation for some unknown reason.

On that Friday at noon, I was to meet three other men at our local church in Lauderdale Lakes and then drive from there to the conference center in Leesburg, Florida. For several days prior to the retreat I was plotting and scheming, trying to come up with some way to get out of this commitment. Finally, I called an old drinking buddy in Orlando and suggested that this would be a most opportune time for us to discuss a languishing business venture and to "shoot it up" for a weekend. Our plan was to meet at his office at 5:30 p.m. that same evening.

But upon my arrival at the church, the other three men, whom I was meeting for the first time, proposed that we all travel together in one vehicle. I protested, suggesting that I follow them alone in my car, since I had some dictation to do for my secretary. Of course, I was lying, but I needed some excuse, along with my wheels, to engage in my extracurricular activity. Nevertheless, they seemed to understand and off we went in separate cars to the campground.

As I was following their car up the Florida Turnpike, I purposely and gradually fell back from them and then eventually turned into a service center. I figured that since they couldn't turn around on the turnpike, they would probably pull off the road for a few minutes to wait for me and then continue on to the conference center. So, after an hour or so of hanging out at the service center, believing that my newly found friends were long gone, I "put the pedal to the metal" and took off to Orlando to meet my friend, Wendell. As I was driving, my mind was lusting like a mad dog in a butcher shop over the great time that I was about to have with my old drinking pal.

The Plan Is Foiled

However, as I slowed down onto the exit ramp for the Orlando turnoff, a vehicle came rushing up alongside mine, blasting its horn, with the front-seat passenger motioning me to slow down and follow them. You guessed it—it was my three new acquaintances! Embarrassed and disappointed, I quickly swung back onto the turnpike and followed them on to our destination.

Upon arriving at the camp, my friends exclaimed, "What in the world were you doing?" I replied that I had to relieve myself and in the process lost them.

"You mean it took you an hour, and then you passed us like a shot out of a cannon as we waited along the roadside?" they asked. "Man, we were driving ninety-five miles per hour just to catch up with you! Didn't you see us? Where were you going?"

Sheepishly I responded, "No, I didn't see you guys. I was just trying to catch up with you and when I couldn't, I thought it best to turn around and go home." Of course, and to my shame, I was lying once again. Quickly, I called my friend Wendell in Orlando and told him that I had been delayed and wouldn't get there until about 8 p.m.

Providentially, one of my three newly acquired friends was Walter Perkins, the previously mentioned Eastern Airline pilot. Being a former "flyboy," I became absorbed in conversation with him, forgetting all about Wendell. The next thing I knew we had finished dinner and the camp bell was ringing for the first meeting at 7 p.m. Again, I called my buddy in Orlando, informing him that I would be in around 10 p.m., but would call prior to leaving the camp.

The rest of the story is history, for within the next twenty-four hours I had a divine appointment with the Great Creator who graciously gave this rebel a new heart. Never again would I be the same person, for my old nature had been miraculously replaced by a new nature, just as the Apostle Paul foretold: "If anyone is in Christ, he is a new creation; old things have passed away; behold, all things have become new" (2 Corinthians 5:17, NKJV).

By the way, I didn't meet with my friend Wendell until after the retreat on Sunday afternoon. When I arrived at his home he exclaimed, "Where in the _____ have you been?" I shared with great excitement what had just transpired, saying, "Man, I've just been re-created! I've experienced my second birth! I'm now a new creature in Christ Jesus!" After listening to my testimony, Wendell's wife, with pointed finger, turned to him and said in an admonishing fashion, "Wendell, that's exactly what *you* need!"

The Enabling Work of the Spirit

The purpose of sharing this anecdote is to emphasize again that if any man is left to himself, he will never find his way to eternal life. But God is sovereign and "desires all men to be saved and to come to the knowledge of the truth." Man is so depraved, so settled in his sin, that he cannot possibly extricate himself from his bondage, come to Christ and believe, unless he receives divine assistance. Jesus emphatically taught this truth in His discourse to the unbelieving masses at Capernaum, when He declared, "No one can come to me unless the Father has *enabled* him" (John 6:65).

This *enabling* work, which is first initiated by the Father through the Spirit, is done both *externally* and *internally* in the unbeliever's life. In other words, God sovereignly designs the circumstances in such a way as to make it possible for a sinner to come to Him.

This was clearly illustrated in my own life, *externally*, through the invitation to attend that men's retreat and the thwarting of my carnal plans with my friend Wendell. Furthermore, God providentially replaced the speaker for that retreat (a very liberal minister) at the last moment with the venerable Dr. Bill Bright. As mentioned previously, Bill's message centered upon broken fellowship with Christ, but it also included the issue of salvation through Christ. My friend, that was no coincidence but exclusively the sovereign grace of a most compassionate and loving God!

The Drawing of the Spirit

In addition to this external work of God, He also does that most important work of *internally enabling* the heart. This work of the Spirit is necessary to overcome what theologians call the *total depravity* of man: "You were dead in your transgressions and sins, in which you used to live when you followed the ways of this world" (Ephesians 2:1-2). If one is *"dead"* spiritually, his heart cannot possibly be resurrected to life unless assisted by some "other power" apart from himself. And this "other power" is exclusively the work of the Holy Spirit. It is done *internally* in such a way as to *convince* one of his sin (as we discussed in chapter 5), change his disposition toward Christ and then make him willing to respond positively to the gospel message.

I wasn't seeking God; I was looking forward to a wild weekend with an old drinking buddy. I was resisting even attending such meetings. But the Spirit of Christ, without my seeking or understanding what was happening, was preparing my heart in such a way as to be *convicted* by the Spirit and then *drawn* to the Savior. This *drawing* of the Spirit is forcefully declared by Jesus in John 6:44: "No one can come to me unless the Father who sent me draws him."

Notice that this verse is very similar to what Jesus expressed previously in a positive fashion, "All that the Father gives me will come to me" (John 6:37). But here it is expressed even more sharply, in negative language, again implying that no one can come to Christ apart from the enabling work of God on his behalf.

In the original text the word *draw* means "to compel by irresistible superiority." It is the same word that is used in describing the *dragging* of fishing nets (John 21:11) and the same word used in portraying Paul and Silas being *dragged* before the authorities in Philippi (Acts 16:19). Also, it's the same word the Greeks use to describe the gravitational pull of the earth. Curiously, this word also "implies resistance to the power that draws."[1] For man does resist, as was the case with both Jeff and me. However, "there is not one single example in the New Testament of the use of this verb where the resistance was successful. Always, the drawing power is triumphant."[2]

So, this pulling or "drawing" is not some "tender wooing" of the Spirit that cooperates with man's volition. To the contrary, it is an *inward and compelling tug* of the Holy Spirit that not only enlightens the heart of sinful man, but also makes willing those who were formerly unwilling and recalcitrant.

The Apostle Paul refers to this as the "sanctifying work of the Holy Spirit." Notice how he states it in Second Thessalonians 2:13: "But we ought always to thank God for you . . . because from the beginning God chose you to be saved through the sanctifying work of the Spirit and through belief in the truth."

I like to think of this "sanctifying work of the Spirit" (that moment of regeneration) in terms of God drawing a circle around the unbeliever and saying, "It's now your time!" One cannot possibly resist this supernatural power of the Spirit, for it is the same power that lifted the ascended Christ from the grave and placed Him at the right hand of God the Father!

This is precisely what happened in both Jeffrey's life and my life. For years we were both hostile to the truth and consumed with the ways of this world, but in God's time and by His *irresistible grace,* He orchestrated both the *external* circumstances and the *internal* condition of our lives in such a way as to bring us—*willingly,* and *not reluctantly*—to faith in Christ!

One Holy Spirit Is Enough; God Doesn't Need Two!

Many times, out of our ignorance to these compelling truths, we attempt to do the work of the Holy Spirit by trying desperately to orchestrate the circumstances for our loved ones, or even our neighbors, to come to Christ.

I have a dear friend in Texas who has quite a testimony relating to this issue. My friend was gloriously saved about the same time that I repented and believed in Christ. He likewise had a drinking problem, along with his wife. In fact, both of them belonged to Alcoholics Anonymous (AA).

Following his conversion, he would raise havoc at the AA meetings by telling the attendees they needed to repent and place their faith specifically in Jesus, the Son of God, not just in some generic "higher being." Every time it was his turn to share in their group meetings, he would invariably focus on the supernatural power of Christ to change the hearts of sinners. Eventually, the others bristled at the mere mention of the name Jesus and finally prohibited him from attending their meetings. Likewise, his wife became hostile and hardened toward his constant talking about the Savior.

But my friend wouldn't let up. He knew all his wife's problems could be solved if she would only repent and believe in Christ. In fact, he would place evangelistic tracts all around the house: under her pillow, in her dresser drawers, in the pockets of her clothing, in books that she was reading, in the silverware drawers, in the dishwasher, in the front seat of her car, etc. You name it and he would place a tract there. But instead of her mellowing toward the gospel, she became even more hardened.

Finally, after a few years of this aggressive evangelism, he took advantage of a new opportunity that he knew for sure would be the right setting for her to accept Christ. So, one evening prior to this scheduled event he asked her, "Precious, how would you like to go down to the Hilton for dinner this coming Saturday night?" She excitedly agreed to go. But what he didn't tell her was that this was the annual dinner of the Christian Business Men's Committee (CBMC) in which the men would bring their wives and others to hear the gospel message.

Saturday evening came and they made their way to the Hilton Hotel. Upon entering the lobby, there was a large sign that read, "Welcome, Wives of CBMC." With this, she turned on her heels and stormed out of the hotel, saying to my friend, "You've done it again; you've lied to me! Get over this Jesus stuff!"

Tragically, the story doesn't end there; in the ensuing days she filed for divorce on the issue of "irreconcilable differences" and eventually the marriage was dissolved. I'll never forget what my dear friend had to say after all of this was over: "Unfortunately, I was trying to play the role of the Spirit. I guess one Holy Spirit is enough; God doesn't need two!"

What, then, should we do about our unsaved family and friends?

First, we must love them and walk faithfully in the power of the Holy Spirit and by His grace become living translations of the gospel. Concurrently, we must be praying fervently for these lost souls. Then, as God gives opportunities to share our faith, we should present the gospel message in a winsome way, being mindful that evangelism is simply "one beggar sharing with another beggar where to find bread."[3]

Perhaps the most difficult mission field in the entire world is one's own family, often because of our inconsistencies and our overzealous desire to "win them" to Christ. Also, we can become immensely discouraged by what we see and hear. Therefore, it behooves us to spend much time in the secret closet of prayer, appealing to the Sovereign One to grant us much grace and wisdom as we cry out to Him to *draw* our lost loved ones—as well as others—unto Himself. And in so doing, we should be encouraged that the Holy Spirit can *convict, convince and draw* men and women unto Himself. Thus, we need not despair of anyone, no matter how rebellious, no matter how self-satisfied, no matter how indifferent. The "Hound of the heavenlies" *can* and *will, by God's amazing grace*, draw sinners unto Himself!

The following prayer is similar to what both Anastasia and I prayed for Jeffrey over the years:

> *Oh, Sovereign One, will You not do for Jeff what he is incapable of doing for himself? You have declared that no one can come to You unless the Father who sent You draws him. So, precious Savior, through that convicting and convincing power of the Spirit, we beg that You would orchestrate the circumstances in Jeff's life, both externally and internally, to make him desperate for You. Then, by Your*

sovereign grace, cause him to willingly respond to the compelling tug, the drawing, of the Holy Spirit.

Oh, Master, could this be that glorious day of his divine appointment with You? By faith and with great expectancy, we thank You in advance, knowing that You do "not ignore the cry of the afflicted" (Psalm 9:12). We pray this in the most worthy name of Jesus! Amen.

SEVEN

For this son of mine was dead and is alive again, he was lost and is found.

Repentance

With *regeneration* being initiated through the *convicting* and *convincing power* of the Holy Spirit, the Comforter now *draws* the sinner to *repentance*—that part of the equation that gives so many, including Satan, a bitter and burning discomfort. So, would it not be the masterstroke of the Pernicious One to attempt to downsize the word *repentance* by replacing it with another word, or eliminating it altogether, so as to impair the biblical doctrine of salvation and weaken the Church? Sadly, this has happened very subtly over time.

Think with me for a moment. If there were to be a sudden outbreak of physical handicaps among newborn infants across our nation, wouldn't you think the Surgeon General of the United States would declare a state of emergency? Absolutely! Our government would harness every available resource: medical and pharmaceutical researchers, biotechnologists and genetic research companies alike, working around the clock to determine the cause and find a cure.

In reality, there is an even more sinister disease, of epidemic proportions, that has swept across our land. Not a physical disease, but a *spiritual disease* that has permeated and weakened the Church. Specifically, it has afflicted multitudes of "new babes" at the time of their presumed spiritual birth by leaving them handicapped with *unregenerate* hearts. Instead of a national emergency, this has become a national scandal as untold numbers of these "new babes" have become "professors of a religion" instead of genuine disciples of Christ Jesus. This has been confirmed by national polls that indicate millions who profess to be "Christians," while their lives abound with self-sufficiency, unforgiveness, greed, malice, pornography, fornication, adultery, homosexuality, pedophilia and other moral and social ills. In fact, this has become so widespread that one secular journalist lamented, "Just at the time when we needed the Church the most, it has become like us!"

And what has caused this wretched epidemic? It is due, in part, to the proclamation of an *incomplete* gospel!

What Is This "Incomplete Gospel"?

I vividly recall one evening, soon after I had become a Christian, lining up my three sons on their knees, next to my bed, and proceeding to lead them through the plan of salvation. They responded in the affirmative by praying "to receive Christ" as their Savior. Joyously, I embraced them and declared, "All is well with you, for now you are Christians—you believe in Jesus Christ!"

Jeffrey was about twelve years of age when this occurred. As was said previously, he was a wonderful young lad, teachable, photogenic, a good student and generally obedient with only occasional tantrums—a normal boy. He was active in Cub Scouts, school activities and the youth group at our local church where he was eventually selected as an "elder." However, as he approached his senior year in high school, those occasional bursts of anger in earlier years became more frequent and pronounced. I attempted to explain this away by thinking, "This is only natural as a child transitions from *dependence* to *independence—growth pains for teenagers*."

Unfortunately, things got worse upon his entering college. It seemed like he was going down the same pathway as his father, as he "set off for a distant country" and engaged in wasted and "wild living" (Luke 15:13). It was in this "far country" that Jeff succumbed to homosexuality. There was a very noticeable change of his attitude, focus and behavior. He seemed distant and indifferent. As I would probe with questions concerning these issues, his responses would be cloaked with flippancy, disgust and anger that eventually led to his declaring, "I hate you and want nothing to do with you!"

It was during this period, his late teenage years and early twenties, that I questioned the whole notion of his "receiving Christ" as a young lad. I mused, "How can a son who professes to be a Christian have such hatred toward his father, let alone engage in a behavior that is so repugnant to God?" It was through the teaching of my mentor, the late J. Edwin Orr, that I discovered the problem. To my chagrin, I had shared with my boys an *incomplete* gospel. Regrettably, out of ignorance, I had downsized the truth by excluding any mention of the *first word* of the gospel.

What Is the First Word of the Gospel?[1]

"It is interesting to notice," Orr wrote in one of his books, "the variety of responses when people are asked: 'What is the first word of the Good News of Jesus Christ?' Some say, 'Only believe.' Others say, 'Love'; 'Hope'; 'Heaven'; 'Liberty'; and a few say, 'Civil Rights.' It was one man's protest that, 'The gospel is so rich in its meaning that it is not possible to state a first word; it has many words of influence.' "[2]

Orr returned to Scripture for an answer to his question, and this was his conclusion:

> If the first word out of the mouth of John the Baptist were the first word out of the mouth of the Lord Jesus, if that were the first word out of the mouth of the twelve disciples, and if that were the first word of the Lord's final instructions to His disciples, and if that were the first word of exhortation out of the mouth of the Apostle Peter in his first sermon at Pentecost, and if that were the first word of the Apostle Paul throughout his ministry, could we not say that this would be the first word of the gospel?[3]

So, what was that first word out of the mouth of John the Baptist? The tax collector, Matthew, records it with clarity in his Gospel message: "In those days came John the Baptist preaching in the wilderness of Judea, saying, 'Repent, for the kingdom of heaven is at hand!' " (Matthew 3:2, NKJV). Again, what was that *first* word?

Next, we find our Lord Jesus on the threshold of His preaching ministry in Galilee. Notice that He dwells upon the very same subject that John had preached; in fact, it "was indeed the sum and substance of all His preaching"[4]: "From that time Jesus began to preach and to say, 'Repent, for the kingdom of heaven is at hand' " (4:17, NKJV).

Had the Lord Jesus preached this before? Apparently not. Was this then His first message? Indeed. And what was its first word? Unequivocally, it was the word *repent*. And immediately following this, our Lord clearly stated His purpose in coming to earth—to save sinners by calling them to *repentance*: "For I did not come to call the righteous, but sinners, to repentance" (9:13, NKJV).

And, most significantly, in our Lord's last discourse with His disciples, He declared, "This is what is written: The Christ will suffer and rise from the dead on the third day, and *repentance* and forgiveness of sins will be preached in his name to all nations, beginning at Jerusalem. You are witnesses of these things" (Luke 24:46-48).

Let me emphasize that this Scripture constitutes the Great Commission every bit as much as the more frequently quoted one in Matthew 28:19-20.

The Apostles' Response

To the glory of God, the apostles faithfully carried out this final commission given to them by the Messiah. After the apostles were filled with the Holy Spirit at Pentecost, and at the conclusion of the very first gospel sermon ever preached, the unbelievers who heard this message cried out, "What shall we do?" Peter responded, "*Repent* and be baptized [i.e., believe], every one of you, in the name of Jesus Christ for the forgiveness of your sins" (Acts 2:38).

And again, in his second message, the apostle boldly declared to the masses, "*Repent* . . . and be converted, that your sins may be blotted out, so that times of refreshing may come from the presence of the Lord" (3:19, NKJV).

When Paul preached to the Epicureans and the Stoic philosophers of Athens he preached a similar message: "But now [God] commands all people everywhere to *repent*" (17:30).

Furthermore, in his powerful testimony before King Agrippa, Paul testified to what he had always preached from the beginning of his ministry, to Jews and Gentiles alike: "I preached that they should *repent* and turn to God and *prove their repentance by their deeds*" (26:20).

The clear implication from these texts, as well as many others, is that these first-century disciples were faithful in preaching the first word of the gospel—*repentance*—to the masses!

What Is Repentance?

This first word of the gospel, *repentance*, with all of its importance, occurs more than fifty times throughout the New Testament. Therefore, we should look at it closely and then define it. It comes from a two-part Greek word, *metanoia*—*meta*, meaning "*change*," and *noia*, meaning "*mind*"—conveying the idea of "a revolution of thought." It has an intellectual as well as a moral impact that can best be summed up in the following definition:

> To feel such regret over one's sins (i.e., "godly sorrow") as to bring about a revolutionary change of *mind*, leading to a radical change of *attitude* and a reformed *behavior*.

Notice the sequence of the definition: *mind, attitude, behavior*. In order for one's *behavior* to be changed, it must first be preceded by a change of *attitude*. And for the *attitude* to be changed, it must be preceded by a *revolutionary change of mind*. Obviously, we can never change a person's mind. We cannot rely on our skills or eloquence to persuade people, but only on the convicting power of the Holy Spirit to bring unbelievers to *repentance*. The old adage mentioned previously still applies: "A person convinced against his will is of the same opinion still." But when the irresistible power of the Spirit descends upon a soul by drawing him to the Master, that person's mind, attitude and behavior will be changed instantly—for all eternity!

Preaching repentance is not a "works" trip, as some suggest; it is simply being faithful to Scripture and trusting the Spirit of Christ to do His convicting work. This is what brings about repentance and regeneration of the sinner. For the Christian message to be *life-changing*, it must first be *mind-altering*. And this mind-altering work is done exclusively by the convicting power of the Holy Spirit through *repentance*. It is accomplished by God's sovereign grace when we present the *complete* gospel, which calls the sinner to *repent and believe* in Jesus Christ.

Because of my ignorance of this most important truth, I had failed to emphasize or even mention this issue of repentance when sharing the gospel with my boys. The "good news" that I had shared was only *"believe in Christ,"* and that is what all three of them did. They believed *intellectually* with their brains, but not *experientially* with their hearts—there was no transformation of mind, attitude or behavior. Yes, they were good boys, but they were mere "professors of the Christian religion."

I recall my friend Edwin Orr saying, "When you share the gospel without including the need of repentance, there is the distinct possibility that the cause of Christ could be set back decades in that person's life." Tragically, I have seen this within my own family and the consequences have been horrific.

The Mickey Cohen Story[5]

It is sad to say that repentance is the missing note in much of our contemporary evangelism. The appeal is not so much for repentance and a new life in Christ, as it is for *enlistment*. In the early 1950s, the notorious gambler, Mickey Cohen, was invited to attend the Hollywood Christian Actors Guild meeting, chaired by the late J. Edwin Orr. A young man named Billy Graham was the speaker. At the conclusion of his message, Mr. Graham gave an invitation and Cohen expressed an interest. Later, a friend of Orr's urged Cohen to invite Jesus Christ into his life by quoting Revelation 3:20—"Here I am! I stand at the door and knock. If anyone hears my voice and opens the door, I will come in and eat with him, and he with me." Cohen professed to do so, but the issue of repentance was neglected.

A few weeks later Orr's friend invited Cohen to hear Mr. Graham speak in Madison Square Garden. As Billy began to preach on the necessity of *repentance* for salvation, Cohen got up and stormed out of the meeting with his would-be spiritual mentor trailing behind him in bewilderment. When asked why he was so upset, Cohen responded, "You didn't tell me that I would have to give up my work [i.e., the rackets]! You didn't tell me I had to give up my friends [i.e., his criminal associates]! You've told me about these Christian athletes, Christian cowboys, Christian actresses—all I wanted to be was a 'Christian gangster.' "[6]

We may laugh at this story, but sadly our churches have become polluted with so-called "Christian adulterers," "Christian gamblers" and "Christian prevaricators." In 1990 a Christian research organization conducted a survey in a well-known megachurch, with 6,000 "believers" in attendance. They were asked questions about their behavior during the six-month period immediately prior to the survey. The following were the results: *at least* one out of eight (approximately thirteen percent) had committed adultery, fornication or homosexual acts; twenty-seven percent had viewed pornography; at least fifty-one percent had been engaged in sexual fantasies (another ten percent refused to answer the question); twenty percent had gambled; eighteen percent had stolen supplies from their employers; fifteen percent had been drunk; thirty-three percent had lied; and only fifty-six percent had read their Bibles.

What Is the Evidence of a Second Birth?

The *only* evidence of a new birth is a new and biblically fruitful life. This fundamental doctrine of salvation is clearly espoused by the Apostle Paul in his second letter to the Corinthians. After stating that he regarded Jesus as a mere man prior to his conversion, he then declares the momentous transformation of one who repents and places his faith in Christ: "Therefore, if anyone is in Christ, he is a new creation; the old has gone, the new has come!" (2 Corinthians 5:17).

If one professes to be a Christian, he should be a new creature—not only in name, but most significantly in heart and in nature. So great is this regenerating grace of God that it creates a whole new world in the soul. The old things are passed away—the old thoughts, old principles, old practices are gone and are replaced with a new mind, new principles, new standards and new company. It is not that one becomes perfect, but he is delivered from the control of the sinful nature and empowered by the Holy Spirit to live by the new nature.

However, if one professes to be a believer but remains in darkness (i.e., loves the world and walks in its ways), in all probability there has been a defect at the time of his so-called "spiritual birth"—*the absence of repentance.* This was the case with Jeffrey at the age of twelve and likewise with myself at the age of twelve. We must remember what Jesus taught: "I have come into the world as a light, so that no one who believes in me should stay in darkness" (John 12:46).

Dr. Orr put the issue succinctly and clearly: "It is quite impossible to truly believe without repenting. The difference between true faith and what the Scripture calls false faith is simple: it is the lack of true repentance."[7] *Faith which is not preceded by repentance and not followed by obedience is not biblical faith*, regardless of what one professes. The plumb line of Scripture reveals the true nature of the heart: "If we claim to have fellowship with him yet walk in the darkness, we lie and do not live by the truth" (1 John 1:6).

How Then Shall We Pray?

We must learn to pray with the Word in our hands and the Spirit in our hearts; here again, we have the case for Scripture praying. The following prayer is similar to what Anastasia and I had prayed for years, but particularly on that Friday evening en route to be with Jeffrey for those final hours of his life:

> Almighty God, we beg that You would extend Your mercy and grace into the life of our son, Jeffrey Scott Burr. We pray that the convicting and convincing power of Your Spirit would so overcome him that the eyes of his heart would be opened and that he would come to his senses and genuinely repent of his sin.

> *Oh Lord, will you not give Jeff the heart of a little boy? You have said, "Unless you change [i.e., repent] and become like little children, you will never enter the kingdom of heaven" (Matthew 18:3). You know he is incapable of changing apart from Your mercy and grace. So, do what You came to earth to do, oh precious Savior—"to save sinners" (1 Timothy 1:15). Grant him a repentant heart by re-creating his mind, attitude and behavior. And then lead him to unshakable faith in You.*
>
> *Thank You for hearing the desperate cry of this father and his wife, for we pray in the most powerful name of Jesus! Amen.*

Forty hours later, with all glory given to the Triune God, Jeffrey repented and anchored his faith in Jesus. For thirty-eight years he had been a mere "professor of a religion"; now he was a genuine disciple of Christ Jesus. He had become a new creation; the old had passed away and the new had come!

Edwin Orr was right in saying, "When you share the gospel absent repentance, there is the potential of setting the cause of Christ back decades in that person's life, if not for all eternity." Therefore, may we cease adhering to an incomplete message and return to declaring the *complete* gospel—*repent and believe!*

EIGHT

For this son
of mine was dead
and is
alive again,
he was lost
and is found.

Praying in Faith

ast, but certainly not least, we come to the most crucial ingredient of effective prayer: faith. This is a faith that trusts in the deity of our sovereign Christ; a faith that believes in His unerring Word; a faith that is persuaded that He has the power and authority to do what He came to earth to do: "to seek and to save that which was lost" (Luke 19:10, NKJV). It is the type of faith that Scripture defines as, "being sure of what we hope for and certain of what we do not see" (Hebrews 11:1). The Greek word literally means "to be confident, persuaded, convinced, sure, won over, trusting in; to believe and to have faith in."

One of the most compelling testimonies that I have ever heard, which truly exemplifies this type of faith, comes from Anastasia's family. Both of her grandparents were Greeks whose families had been taken captive by the Ottoman Empire during the nineteenth century and held in Turkey. In the latter part of that century, American missionaries residing in Athens were supernaturally allowed to enter that thoroughly Muslim country to feed and clothe the poor and, very subtly, share the gospel. It was in this environment that many of these Greek exiles trusted in Christ Jesus and became evangelical Christians. Among them was Anastasia's grandmother, Sultana.

In 1910 Sultana married a Greek man by the name of Ignatios Meletiadis. In 1912 they had their first and only child, Lydia, who eventually became Anastasia's mother. In that same year, the Ottoman Empire set about to conscript all male Greek captives into their army. Realizing that the Greeks were among the many enemies of the Turks and, having no stomach to fight against his own people, Ignatios, along with a few other young men, stealthily slipped out of their village under the cloak of darkness and escaped. Upon arriving at Istanbul, Ignatios was offered passage on a Greek vessel destined for the United States. His plan was to earn some money and, within a few short years, bring his wife and daughter to America.

The Prodigal Grandfather

Upon arriving in this country Ignatios found work in the coal mines of eastern Pennsylvania, then migrated to western Pennsylvania and eventually to the upper Midwest. Sadly, he drifted into the ways of the world and eventually became an alcoholic, living the life of a bum. After his first five years in the United States, his family, still captives in Turkey, no longer heard from him.

In 1924, following the defeat of the Ottoman Empire, the governments of Greece and Turkey finally agreed to an exchange of their ethnic populations. Sultana and Lydia, along with other relatives and friends, returned to Greece. In 1926, Lydia was married and eventually had six children, with Anastasia being the youngest.

Still there was no word from Ignatios. Ten years went by, then twenty, thirty, forty, fifty—yet not a word from the prodigal husband and father. However, Anastasia recalls most vividly the vibrancy and depth of her grandmother's faith; she was resolute in praying for her long-lost husband throughout those many decades. Not until 1972 did word come to the family that Ignatios was still alive and thought to be living in Ohio.

Immediately, Anastasia's brother, Constantine, flew to America in search of the old man. By God's grace, he found the intemperate centenarian living in a rundown tenement house in Massillon, Ohio. Ignatios was now 100 years old and had not been seen by his wife and family for some sixty years! After convincing Ignatios that he was really his grandson, Constantine took him to his motel, gave him a bath (he was grossly unkempt), bought him a set of new clothes, purchased a one-way airline ticket to Greece and put a roll of $20 bills in his pocket—for a Greek never returns home without bearing gifts!

At the airport in Thessaloniki, Sultana and her entire clan were waiting breathlessly for the return of their prodigal husband, father and grandfather. There was much excitement and tears of joy as Ignatios stepped off the plane—even the security guards got caught up in all the emotion!

At the family home in Mylotopos they "killed the fattened calf" and had a community-wide celebration. Relatives and family friends from both near and far came to show their love to Ignatios. He was thoroughly overwhelmed by this effusive display of affection and generous reception.

After several days of Ignatios constantly asking, "How can you possibly show me such love? How can God, and you, possibly forgive me for what I've done to you?" Sultana replied, "Because of the love of Jesus, who came into this world for sinners like you and me!" Then his daughter Lydia, Anastasia's mother, shared with him the gospel. At once the convicting power of the Spirit descended upon the old man; he dropped to his knees, crying out to God for forgiveness, *repenting* and *believing* in the Lord Jesus Christ. He was gloriously regenerated—re-created into a totally new man in Christ—at the ripe old age of 100! With an incredibly keen mind for his age (particularly after decades of intemperance) and a clear conscience, *Pappous* (Greek for "Grandpa") Ignatios lived another seven years—the best years of his life—until the Lord finally took him home.

The Power of Faith

This story demonstrates not only the unfathomable mercy and grace of our loving God, but also the efficacy of *unwaver-*

ing faith as modeled by a precious wife and her family. Never once did Sultana think about divorce, but truly believed that her merciful Savior would rescue her wayward husband from the dregs of the world. This is precisely the kind of faith that Jesus spoke about in Mark 11:22-25 as He was making His way into Jerusalem for the final hours of His earthly life and ministry.

The context of our Lord's teaching takes place on the Tuesday morning of Passion Week. As He, along with His disciples, was returning to Jerusalem from Bethany they saw the withered remains of the fig tree that Jesus had cursed the previous day (11:14). The disciples were stunned by the awesome display of His *power* and *authority*, for the destruction of the tree appeared to be much more severe than the curse. This prompted Peter to exclaim, "Rabbi, look! The fig tree you cursed has withered!" (11:21).

Without explaining the significance of the curse (i.e., the impending judgment of Israel), Jesus uses this occasion to connect this spectacle of His *power* with instruction about the *object* of one's faith. Because the source of such power rests totally in God, He enjoins them in verse 22 to "have faith in God."

In other words, for faith to be dynamic it must *always* be anchored upon our triune God and not in something we can feel, touch or see in the physical realm. And this was exactly the case with Sultana—her persevering faith was riveted upon the omnipotent Messiah and the truthfulness of His word. The Word of God had instructed her, "Christ Jesus came into the world to save sinners" (1 Timothy 1:15) . . . "not wanting anyone to perish, but everyone to come to repentance" (2 Peter 3:9) and "he rewards those who earnestly seek him" (Hebrews 1:6). It was on these truths that she fixed her faith, "being sure of what [she] hope[d] for and certain of what [she did] not see" (11:1) and never allowing any form of *doubt* to undercut her belief in Christ.

The Power of Prayer

Jesus continues His discourse by connecting such *power* and *faith* with one's communion with God. The kind of faith He is referring to generates an "affectionate outreach of one's mind for God," which is expressed through *prayer* to the God of all miracles. Since He and His disciples were standing on the Mount of Olives, from which the Dead Sea could be seen on a clear day, He uses this awe-inspiring occasion to speak figuratively about "mountain-moving" prayer. The term *mountain* here implies obstacles that are perceived as immovable; things that appear to be impossible with man, but are nevertheless possible with God (Mark 10:27). Notice the solemnity with which He begins his statement in 11:23: "I tell you the truth"; this phrase is used to emphasize the importance of the rest of His statement: "If anyone says to this mountain, 'Go, throw yourself into the sea,' and does not doubt in his heart but believes that what he says will happen, it will be done for him."

This is not some form of "Praying" in which the supplicant works himself up into some type of emotional self-intoxication; it is a calm assurance that is anchored in the faithfulness of God and the promises of His Word.

Sultana had developed a steadfast and resolute faith in God that was based exclusively upon His Word. It was a faith that did not entertain doubt, but moved the "mountains" of her life. This type of believing prayer is to *believe* that one has already *received* what they have requested even though the answer is still in the future. Notice how the Lord Jesus exhorts His disciples with this mind-bending principle and promise in verse 24: "Therefore I tell you, whatever you ask for in prayer [present tense], believe that you have received it [past tense], and it will be yours [future tense]."

Once again, I want to emphasize that one's assurance in Praying for lost souls must rest exclusively upon: (1) our all-powerful and loving God, (2) His faithfulness to His Word and (3) the promises thereof. Since we are instructed that "Christ Jesus came into the world to save sinners" (1 Timothy 1:15) . . . "not wanting anyone to perish, but everyone to come to repentance" (2 Peter 3:9), we can then pray and thank the Author of these statements in advance for what He will do in the future! And this is a demonstration of *great faith!*

Hindrances to Believing Prayer

I hasten to add, however, that there are two subtle hindrances which can negate the above promise. The first is *doubt*, as mentioned by our Master in Mark 11:23. Doubt never comes from God, but from the residue of our old sinful nature, which always wars against our new nature in Christ (Galatians 5:17) by coiling around our hearts like a boa constrictor to capitalize upon the adverse circumstances of our lives.

One of the chief purposes of Satan, assisted by the sinful nature, is to thwart our faith in God by creating discouragement and doubt, thus making God's powerful promises and truths ineffectual in our lives. "He who doubts is like a wave of the sea, blown and tossed by the wind. That [kind of person] should not think he will receive anything from the Lord; he is a double-minded man, unstable in all he does" (James 1:6-8).

An Unforgiving Heart

The other hindrance that Jesus speaks about in this passage of Scripture is *forgiveness*. Notice the warning and command He gives in Mark 11:25: "And when you stand

Praying, if you hold anything against anyone, forgive him, so that your Father in heaven may forgive you your sins."

It may appear that the transition from verse 24 to verse 25 is somewhat abrupt, but there is a very definitive connection between the two. Forgiveness toward others is directly tied to the divine forgiveness that we Christians have received from God. Just as the Father was magnanimous in extending His unfathomable love toward us through His forgiveness, we are likewise commanded (*commanded*, not suggested) to be generous in extending this forgiving love to others—unbelievers and believers alike.

Invariably, this becomes the acid test of our faith, trust, hope and belief in God. To the praise of the Almighty, *Yaya* (Greek for "Grandma") Sultana excelled in this quality. She could have been extremely bitter and resentful, but her faith was coupled with an appreciation of her own forgiveness from God. Someone has said, "Forgiveness is the fragrance the violet sheds on the heel that crushed it," and this was very well the case with Sultana. The fragrance of her heart was a forgiving spirit.

But, if the attitude of one's heart is *not* inclined to forgive, then God will not forgive him for his sins, because *he has just burned the bridge over which he himself must pass* (see Matthew 6:15). This type of attitude becomes a major hindrance to answered prayer.

Therefore, we should examine ourselves by asking: "What is the object of my faith? Do I *really* believe in Jesus? Is He my Savior and Lord? If so, what is the fragrance of my heart? Who is that person I have not forgiven? Is it possible that this person has not come to repentance and faith in Christ because of *my* attitude—*my* impenitence?" With these thoughts in mind, may I suggest the following prayer as an attempt to keep our fragile souls in proper relationship with God as we engage in Praying for unbelievers?

> *Father God, I thank You for extending Your lovingkindness to me, a sinner, through the death of Your glorious Son, Jesus Christ. And thank You, O Lamb of God, for enduring that excruciating pain of the Cross to personally rescue me from my depravity through the shedding of Your precious blood.*
>
> *As You have been magnanimous in extending Your mercy and grace to me, I now ask that You, O Spirit of Christ, would search my heart for anything that has contaminated and/or broken my fellowship and communion with You. As You show me my sin, including any hint of unforgiveness or any form of doubting Your character and Word, I pledge to confess it and repent thereof.*
>
> (Pause and now ask the Spirit to search your heart; after you confess and repent of your sin, continue.)
>
> *Lord, by faith, fill me afresh and anew with Your blessed Holy Spirit!*
>
> *Now, O gracious Redeemer, I ask that through the convicting power of the Holy Spirit You would extend Your mercy and grace to [name of unbeliever]. Forgive him for what he has done, for surely he doesn't realize the pain he has caused You and others. Create within him a spirit of repentance with a cleansed heart.*
>
> *O sovereign Christ, I humbly remind You that Your coming to earth was "to save sinners . . . not wanting anyone to perish, but everyone to come to repentance." Therefore, by faith in You and Your unfailing Word, I thank You in advance for that day in which [name of unbeliever] will repent and place his faith in You!*
>
> *Lord Jesus, could this be the day when my prodigal comes home? It is in Your most gracious name that I pray. Amen.*

In closing this book, my heart is overcome with the tender mercies of our gentle Shepherd as He calls prodigals, sinners, to come "home." The profound lyrics of Will Thompson's invitational hymn "Softly and Tenderly" (1880) expresses it most passionately:

> Softly and tenderly Jesus is calling,
>   Calling for you and for me;
> See on the portals He's waiting and watching,
>   Watching for you and for me.
>
> Come home, come home,
>   Ye who are weary, come home,
> Earnestly, tenderly Jesus is calling,
>   Calling, O sinner, come home![1]

And the prodigal responded,

> "I will set out and go back to my father and say to him: Father, I have sinned against heaven and against you. I am no longer worthy to be called your son; make me like one of your hired men." So he got up and went to his father.
>
> But while he was still a long way off, his father saw him and was filled with compassion for him; he ran to his son, threw his arms around him and kissed him.
>
> The son said to him, "Father, I have sinned against heaven and against you. I am no longer worthy to be called your son."
>
> But the father said to his servants, "Quick! Bring the best robe and put it on him. Put a ring on his finger and sandals on his feet. Bring the fattened calf and kill it. Let's have a feast and celebrate. For this son of mine was dead and is alive again; he was lost and is found."
>
> (Luke 15:18-24)

To God be the glory—great things He hath done!

Epilogue

hat follows on the next several pages is a basic presentation of the gospel message. In the event that you are not certain of your own spiritual destiny, you are invited to study this message, examine the Scripture verses and then—as the Spirit of Jesus so leads—joyfully surrender your life to Christ.

For those of you who are disciples of the Master, you are encouraged to share this gospel presentation with your own prodigal or another unbeliever, as you are led by the Holy Spirit. Feel free to reproduce these pages and distribute them, as you so desire.

Have You Experienced Your Second Birth?

f not, there is a God-shaped vacuum deep within your heart. For God made you with a space in your inner being that only He can fill.

When God created the human race, it was His *ultimate purpose* that man would glorify Him (Isaiah 43:7) by fulfilling two of His greatest commandments: "Love the Lord your God with all your heart and with all your soul and with all your mind" and "Love your neighbor as yourself" (Matthew 22:37, 39).

Why, then, do so few people seem to achieve this in their lives?

You can be certain that the problem is not with God!

Since God is the Author of life (Genesis 1) and love (1 John 4:16), He made man for the definitive purpose of being His *image bearer* on earth (Genesis 1:26). Therefore, man and woman were created perfectly with a *body* (matter—to live in the material world), a *soul* (personality) and a *spirit* (life with God-consciousness)—three parts in one (1 Thessalonians 5:23). All three were to be thoroughly devoted to Him. This three-part nature is illustrated in the diagram below.

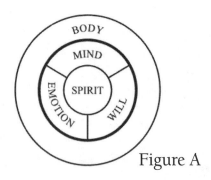

Figure A

Notice that the middle ring, which represents the *soul*, is in turn divided into three parts: the *mind*, the *emotion* and the *will*. God made us with a *mind* (intellect) to understand divine precepts without error, with *emotions* (feelings) to express ourselves without inordinate passions or appetites and with a *will* (freedom of choice) to readily and joyfully comply with the will of God without reluctance or resistance.

Finally, God made us with a *spirit* (the inner circle) to be *spiritual beings*, having a unique relationship with our Creator by excelling in love, communion and obedience to Him for all eternity.

Thus, it was God's *ultimate purpose* that mankind would be His representatives on earth through whom His love, ways and purposes would be reproduced and reflected. As Scripture tells us, we were "created for [His] glory" (Isaiah 43:7)!

With such a lofty origin of the human race in view, the question arises, "Whatever happened to the human race? How could man and woman have wandered so far from the original designs for which God created them?"

The Fall of Mankind

The answer to these compelling questions is found in the third chapter of Genesis where the crafty serpent—the incarnate Satan—used his subtle temptations of *intellectual pride* and *sensual gratification* (Genesis 3:5-6) to deceive our first parents, Adam and Eve. They willfully turned away from God and shifted their allegiance to Satan by (1) disobeying God's command to not eat the forbidden fruit (2:17), (2) believing the lie of Satan, "you will be like God" (3:4-5), which tempted them to pride and (3) placing their own wills above God's will (3:6), which is rebellion.

The consequences of Adam and Eve's actions were horrendous, for they were immediately separated from God (3:23).

The Creator's love and likeness in them was lost. Their consciences became shamed and sullied. Their happiness turned to misery and their comfort was replaced with pain, disease and death. The Creator's light (righteousness) that had been shining brilliantly into their souls was now replaced with darkness as *depravity* overcame their entire being. This depravity is illustrated by the horizontal lines in the diagram below.

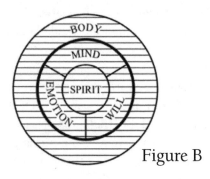

Figure B

This dreadful *original sin* of our first parents became like a cataclysmic earthquake rippling down through the ages, distorting, darkening and corrupting every single soul that was ever to be born, with the *sole* exception of Jesus Christ. This original sin was transferred to the children of Adam through the generative process, from parent to child, making us all fellow participants in Adam's sin. The Bible speaks clearly to this truth:

> Just as sin entered the world through one man [Adam], and death through sin, and in this way death came to all men, because all sinned. (Romans 5:12)

> There is no one righteous, not even one;
>   there is no one who understands,
>   no one who seeks God.
> All have turned away,

> they have together become worthless . . .
> for all have sinned and fall short of the glory of God.
> (Romans 3:10-12, 23)

Therefore, mankind could no longer experience true love and abundant life as God intended it to be. So what is the destiny of sinful man? Is it everlasting separation from God?

Christmas Arrives!

Fortunately, this is not the end of the story. Although fallen man does not seek after God (Romans 3:11; Psalm 14:2-3; Ephesians 2:1), God, in His infinite love, does seek after man. In fact, God has a whole new plan to *re-create* man in the pattern originally set forth in the beginning!

As soon as Satan inflicted his mortal wound on Adam and Eve, our Creator God provided an immediate remedy. He promised to send His *Deliverer* to rescue mankind, to "crush" Satan's head (Genesis 3:14-15). This Savior of the world would then become the sacrificial Lamb of God by taking upon Himself the punishment for our sins. The prophet Isaiah described it this way:

> But he was pierced for our transgressions,
>   he was crushed for our iniquities;
> the punishment that brought us peace was upon him,
>   and by his wounds we are healed. (53:5)

The Savior, Jesus, thus became the perfect sacrifice that would pay the debt for sinful man, for "God made him who had no sin to be sin for us, so that in him we might become the righteousness of God" (2 Corinthians 5:21).

This was the glorious *gift of Christmas*—God's Redeemer for helpless humanity! Just as the Father created light out of darkness by commanding, "Let there be light" (Genesis 1:3), He now sends His Light, the one and only begotten Son of God—Jesus—into this world through the Holy Spirit's over-

shadowing of the Virgin Mary (Luke 1:35). This was to be
God's divine plan for restoring condemned man unto Himself,
that "through [Jesus] all men might believe . . . [for] the true
light that gives light to every man was coming into the world"
(John 1:7, 9).

This was the promise given to the human race:

> Yet to all who received him, to those who believed in his
> name, he gave the right to become children of God—
> children born not of natural descent, nor of human de-
> cision or a husband's will, but born of God. (1:12-13)

But how could helpless man be "born of God" and receive
a "new spirit" when he is "dead in [his] transgressions and
sins" (Ephesians 2:1)?

"You Must Be Born from Above"

Just as the Author of life *created* man from the dust of the
earth by breathing into him the breath of life (Genesis 2:7),
likewise, He is the *only* One who can *re-create* man from his
totally depraved and fallen nature. This *spiritual re-creation*
is God's undeserved favor extended to sinners through the
work of the Holy Spirit. This occurs when one *repents* and
believes the good news of Jesus (Mark 1:15).

Furthermore, Jesus declared: "No one can see the kingdom of God unless he is born again" (John 3:3).

When a person realizes he is guilty of sinning against God
and genuinely repents (turns away from his sin) and places his
faith in Christ Jesus, he is "born from above" or "born again"
(3:3). This is an immediate and supernatural transaction of the
Spirit of Christ as He draws one from spiritual deadness and
depravity into a whole new life—a spiritual re-creation. He is
cleansed instantly from all past, present and future sins. At the
same moment, the Spirit of God supernaturally replaces the
sinner's *old* nature with a *new* nature, as the Holy Spirit takes

up permanent residence within his soul (Romans 8:9-11) and *reconciles* him with God *for all eternity*, as shown in the diagram below.

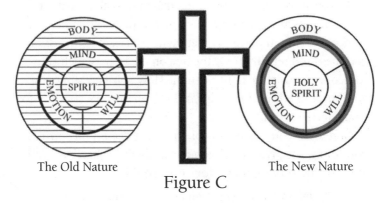

The Old Nature   The New Nature

Figure C

This truth is succinctly expressed in Second Corinthians 5:17: "Therefore, if anyone is in Christ, he is a new creation; the old has gone, the new has come."

Notice in the diagram how Jesus, the Deliverer, acts as a bridge in transferring sinners from *darkness and death* into *fullness of life for all eternity*. For Christ Jesus declared,

> For God so loved the world that he gave his one and only Son, that whoever believes in him shall not perish but have *eternal* life. For God did not send his Son into the world to condemn the world, but to *save the world through him*. (John 3:16-17)

Therefore, Jesus, "the Lamb of God, who takes away the sin of the world" (1:29), is able to accomplish this because God sent Him to be the *only* mediator who can reconcile us with our loving Creator. Scripture instructs us: "For Christ died for sins once for all, the righteous for the unrighteous, to bring you to God" (1 Peter 3:18).

Furthermore, Jesus decreed: "I am the way and the truth and the life. No one comes to the Father except through me" (John 14:6).

As you look over the previous diagram, which of the two circles represents your life? The one on the left, that portrays someone living in darkness, depravity, self-centeredness, ungodliness and rebellion? Or the one on the right, which shows someone living in the light, with the Holy Spirit creating peace and purpose within his heart? Which one would you like to characterize your life?

God loves you, regardless of your past deeds and spiritual condition. His great invitation in Matthew 11:28-29 is available, at this very moment, for your troubled soul:

> Come to me, all you who are weary and burdened, and I will give you rest. Take my yoke upon you and learn from me, for I am gentle and humble in heart, and you will find rest for your souls.

Is it your desire to be *forgiven* of your sins, *re-created* into the image and likeness of our loving God for all of eternity, and to experience the *ultimate purpose of life* for which you were created? If so, then you are invited to pray the following prayer:

> *Almighty God, I acknowledge that I am a sinner. I repent of my wretched deeds and self-serving life. Even though I deserve eternal punishment, I beg for Your mercy and grace. I ask that You cleanse me with the precious blood of Jesus, for I believe He died for me on the cross and rose from the grave, that He paid the penalty for all my sin.*
>
> *I ask that You, Jesus, would become my Lord and Savior of my life and take me as Your adopted child for all of eternity. Cause me to love You with all my heart and to love my neighbor as myself. Help me to live for You through the enabling power of the Holy Spirit.*

> *And, as an act of faith, I thank You for hearing and answering the plea of this repentant sinner. I pray this in the most holy name of Jesus, who is the living and risen Savior of the world and is now my Savior and Lord! Amen.*

If you have sincerely prayed this prayer, you are now a new creature in Christ! The Bible promises, "everyone who calls on the name of the Lord will be saved" (Romans 10:13).

> He who has the Son has life; he who does not have the Son of God does not have life.
>
> I write these things to you who believe in the name of the Son of God so that you may know that you have eternal life. (1 John 5:12-13)

Now that you received your *second birth*, continue in this new life by implementing the following:

1. Read the Bible daily. Immerse your mind in God's Word. A good place to begin with First Peter and then the Gospel of John, both in the New Testament.

2. Learn to pray the Scriptures. This is a most powerful and awesome way to commune with God. Start with Psalm 23. Then move on through the other Psalms and the New Testament. Remember, God speaks to you through His Word. As you read verse by verse, allow the Holy Spirit, who now lives in your heart, to minister to your mind by formulating your prayers. Then respond to God from what He has just said to you through His Word.

3. Join a Christ-centered, Bible-believing church where the entire Bible is preached and taught.

4. Begin sharing with others, in a winsome way, the greatest discovery of your life—*new life in Christ!* Remember, the *ultimate purpose of life* includes being Christ's representative—His *ambassador* on earth—to reach and serve needy and lost souls.

If you would like additional information, visit us on-line at www.ptam.org or write us at:

Pray-Think-Act Ministries, Inc.
P.O. Box 267
New Wilmington, PA 16142 USA

Endnotes

Prologue

1. Ole Hallesby, *Prayer* (Minneapolis: Augsburg, 1994), p. 99.

Chapter 2—Some Cold, Hard Facts

1. Tom Allen, *Hope for Hurting Parents* (Camp Hill, PA: Christian Publications, Inc., 1999), p. 6.
2. Richard Burr, *Developing Your Secret Closet of Prayer* (Camp Hill, PA: WingSpread Publishers, 1998), pp. 154-161.
3. Matthew Henry, *Matthew Henry's Commentary: Job to Song of Solomon, Volume 3* (Grand Rapids, MI: Revel, n.d.), p. 917.
4. Burr, *Developing Your Secret Closet of Prayer.*

Chapter 3—The Role of Prayer

1. Kenneth S. Wuest, *The New Testament: An Expanded Translation* (Grand Rapids, MI: Eerdmans), p. 251.
2. Alexander Whyte, *Lord, Teach Us To Pray* (London, Hodder and Stoughton, 1900). Reprinted, *Classic Sermons on Prayer,* Hendrickson Publishers, Inc.
3. This union of prayer with the Word is known as Scripture Praying. See chapter 5 of my book, *Developing Your Secret Closet of Prayer* (Camp Hill, PA: WingSpread Publishers, 1998).
4. Matthew Henry, *Matthew Henry's Commentary: Genesis to Deuteronomy, Volume 1* (Grand Rapids, MI: Revell, n.d.), p. 411.
5. Wuest, p. 184 (Luke 18:1).
6. J. Ligon Duncan, "A Notable Prayer Meeting," [on-line], n.d. March 14, 2003. Available from: <http://www.reformationsociety.org/preview/notable_prayer_meeting.asp>.

Chapter 4—God Desires All to Be Saved

1. A.W. Pink, *The Nature of God* (Chicago: Moody Press, 1975, 1999), p. 86.
2. John Walvoord & Roy Zook, *The Bible Knowledge Commentary, New Testament Edition* (Wheaton, IL: SP Publications, 1983), p. 733.
3. Pink, p. 74.
4. Charles Colson, *Against the Night* (Ann Arbor, MI: Servant Publications, 1989), pp. 143-145.

Chapter 5—The Convicting Power of the Holy Spirit

1. The next chapter, "The Drawing of the Spirit," will expand upon this issue.

2. James Montgomery Boice, *John, Vol. 4* (Grand Rapids, MI: Baker), p. 1208.
3. Ibid.
4. Matthew Henry, *Matthew Henry's Commentary: Matthew to John, Volume V* (Grand Rapids, MI: Revell, n.d.), p. 1137.
5. R.A. Torrey, *The Person and Work of the Holy Spirit* (Grand Rapids, MI: Zondervan Publishing House, 1978), pp. 71-74.
6. Ibid., p. 75.

Chapter 6—The Drawing of the Spirit

1. James Montgomery Boice, *The Gospel of John, Vol. 2* (Grand Rapids: Baker Books, 1985, 1999), p. 514.
2. Ibid.
3. Charles Haddon Spurgeon (1834-1892).

Chapter 7—Repentance

1. Attribution is given to J. Edwin Orr, *My All, His All* (Wheaton, IL: International Awakening Press, 1989), chapter 1.
2. Ibid., p. 2.
3. Ibid.
4. Matthew Henry, *Matthew Henry's Commentary, Vol. 5* (Peabody, MA: Hendrickson, 1991), p. 41.
5. Orr, p. 7. (Many of the details of this story were given to me directly by the late Dr. Orr.)
6. Ibid.
7. Ibid., p. 8.

Chapter 8—Praying in Faith

1. Will L. Thompson, "Softly and Tenderly," *Hymns of the Christian Life* (Camp Hill, PA: Christian Publications, Inc., 1978), #550.